# JESUS MEANS LIFE

by Harold and Patricia Wells
Engravings by Nancy Ruth Jackson

Division of Communication (CEM)
The United Church of Canada
Toronto, Ontario

Copyright © 1982 Division of Communication (CEM)
The United Church of Canada

ISBN 0-919357-30-X

Publisher: R.C. Plant
Editor: Nancy E. Hardy
Production Editor: Patricia Cook
Typesetting: Lynda Walton

Book design and engravings: Nancy Ruth Jackson

Printed and bound in Canada by
Image Design & Print Ltd.
Hamilton, Ontario

# CONTENTS

APPENDIX

# OUR THANKS

Many people have contributed to the making of this book. We are grateful to the members of the editorial committee and to the readers and test groups who used the first draft and gave us criticisms and suggestions.

We especially want to thank our East Plains test group for their enthusiastic and frank assistance: Joe Atyeo, Norma Bidwell, Art Blair, Susan Cameron, Pat Holmes, Naomi Hurd, Marg James, Cathy Jensen, Estelle Kjarsgaard, Gail Lorimer, Joan Lymburner, Lillian MacLean, Margaret McConnell, Ev Mercer, Pat Vollick, Nelson Watson, Peggy Wright.

Thanks are also due to friends, scholars and colleagues who took pains over the first manuscript, particularly John McTavish, Donna Runnalls, and George Wright.

Finally, many scholars have influenced our thought, but we would like to specifically acknowledge Albert Nolan, a South African theologian, whose book *Jesus Before Christianity* opened our eyes to many things which we would not otherwise have seen.

*Harold and Pat*

# PREPARE FOR SURPRISE

In a book of this kind it seems only fair at the outset to state our bias. We begin with the contention that Jesus' humanity, Jesus as a man of flesh and bone, has since at least the fourth century, been slurred over. Christians have happily recognized his divinity and too often forgotten that he was very much an individual involved in the struggles of his own time.

He was a Jew. He could only have come out of Israel, and could only have been understood by others in that tradition. Much of what he said was not unique. The loving, sacrificial defense of the poor and the ideas of repentance, forgiveness, and atonement were firmly embedded in Jewish faith.

However, what we also believe, both from our living and our reflection, is that Jesus was uniquely and radically filled with God's Spirit, that he was God with us. In his life, death, and in his resurrection, he can show us God as no one else can and so offer us and our broken world a richness of life we only fractionally glimpse. We hope some of the grounds for these beliefs will become evident in the following pages.

We have also written with an ear to the Third World. We would recognize, even emphasize, that Canadians should let the Bible speak to their specific situation and problems, and the thinking of Christians in other places, whether in the United States, Germany or Latin America, can never be swallowed whole. Nevertheless, having lived in southern Africa for some time, we can see how the insights of Third World Christians could be enlightening and corrective to many of our Canadian church emphases. And as members of the global Christian community we have no option but to listen to their concerns.

Finally, we hope that for you this study will not be an academic rehashing of old assumptions but a fresh pilgrimage into faith, that you will be willing to strike out into old lands as though you had never been there before and be prepared to be surprised. We urge you to go back to the gospels and reread them for yourself, as we have had to do in writing this (they're not really very long) and form your own conclusions. It could be that this Jesus is, in fact, in many ways, different from what we have believed.

May God go with you in your search.

*Pat and Harold*

to
Tlohang

"Jesus calls us not to a new religion, but to life."
Dietrich Bonhoeffer

# CHAPTER ONE
# CAN WE KNOW THE REAL JESUS?

Seeing that many others have undertaken to draw up accounts of the events that have taken place among us, exactly as these were handed down to us by those who from the outset were eyewitnesses and ministers of the word, I in my turn, after carefully going over the whole story from the beginning, have decided to write an ordered account for you, Theophilus, so that your Excellency may learn how well founded the teaching is that you have received.

*Luke 1: 1-4*

There were many other signs that Jesus worked and the disciples saw, but they are not recorded in this book. These are recorded so that you may believe that Jesus is the Christ, the Son of God, and that believing this you may have life through his name.

*John 20: 30-31*

## OUR IMAGES OF HIM

In the third form classroom of an African mission high school hangs a picture of a mild-eyed and undoubtedly Anglo-Saxon Jesus. His exposed heart drips with blood, and the students, to our knowledge, have never questioned his authenticity.

On a street in Cuba hangs a life size poster of Jesus in army fatigues, a gun slung over his shoulder. A group of Bolivian high school students, asked who Jesus was, unhesitatingly replied, "For us Jesus Christ is Che Guevara."[1]

The Nicene Creed, formulated in A.D. 325, speaks of him as

the only begotten Son of God
begotten of his Father before all worlds,
God of God, light of light,
very God of very God
begotten not made
being of one substance with the Father
by whom all things were made.

Dietrich Bonhoeffer, a twentieth century theologian and martyr, describes Jesus as "the man for others," and writes, in a letter from a Nazi prison, that in Christ "God lets himself be pushed out of the world on to the Cross. He is weak and powerless in the world, and that is precisely the way, the only way, in which he is with us and helps us."[2]

We give him the accents of our time and our own colouration, probably our own protective colouration. Is it possible that we too easily listen to the Jesus of the gospels as we might listen to a Sunday sermon, approving of what we like and discarding what is disturbing or unclear? Do our images of him too often aid and abet our own social position? The white South African mine supervisor sees him as the bulwark of white civilization and morality, enjoining charity and guaranteeing eternal life. The black African mine labourer sees him either as the consoling friend promising a better life in heaven or as the revolutionary leader, calling people to fight for better living conditions now.

We North Americans tend to brand him the Great Moral Teacher and use him for pediatric purposes. Dousing a child in The Golden Rule is a modest insurance against future criminality and too much "running around." When the teaching is absorbed, the Teacher becomes redundant.

However we may be tempted to use him for our own purposes and create him in our own image, the fact remains that we must see him from some perspective and that can only be our own. We may look at a tree from one angle or another, but we must look at it from some angle; in the same way, we can only see Jesus from the place where we are at this moment standing. We go to him with all we have and are and our minds grope with difficulty back over the centuries to a society where the individual was an integral part of the community, where illness was caused by demons, and where there were no washing machines. But this is not to say that our perception of him need be wildly distorted. We can recognize that we do see him from within our own limitations and yet attempt to keep an open, listening mind, willing to let ourselves be questioned and startled.

Probably in the end, the really astounding fact is not that we have these difficulties, but that we who watch space shuttles are still interested in this carpenter from Nazareth who was executed as a criminal two thousand years ago. By all the laws of logic he ought to have been quietly forgotten. Yet, in spite of all our cultural differences and the distortions of time, he is still there, pulling at us and questioning our neat, convenient images of him.

## THE PROBLEM OF THE HISTORICAL RECORDS

The problem of knowing the real Jesus is further complicated by the type of historical records we have about him. When the early Christians got together in each other's houses they would tell and retell the stories of what Jesus had said and done. Different groups knew different stories or different versions of the same story.

The gospels were written to preserve these oral traditions and to inspire faith. They were used as catechisms and for worship, and bear each writer's interpretations of the events. Each gospel writer has his own perspective on Jesus. Matthew, writing for Jews, frequently refers to the Old Testament and emphasizes Jesus as the expected Messiah. Luke, a physician writing for gentiles, stresses Jesus' compassion for the poor and sees him as the universal Saviour. Mark was a lover of deeds, and John was a lover of theology. The gospels as a whole are most definitely not the consistent, impersonal, chronological and carefully documented accounts we might have liked. In our weaker moments we may wish that God had poured the gospel, word by Greek word, directly into the writers' empty minds and not chosen to let them express their faith freely and be fallible. The inevitable question arises: are the gospels really reliable records of the events? Are they so overlaid with the enthusiasms of their authors and the early church and the kinds of myths and legends that grow up around any powerful personality that they are of questionable value?

For two centuries, these kinds of problems have agitated biblical scholarship and the result has been some very intricate detective work into the gospel texts.

The texts, for example, have been meticulously compared against each other and an attempt made to sort out the different strands of tradition. We now know that Luke and Matthew both had Mark and another common source in front of them when they were writing. Because they had much more material to work into their accounts, they tended to shorten or paraphrase Mark's version. The other written or oral traditions they were using and the people they were writing for also weighed heavily in how they told the story. Matthew, for instance, was writing for a group of people who were not poor or hungry or miserable, and records Jesus saying "Blessed are the poor in spirit." Luke, and probably the Christian community of which he was a part, wanted to preserve Jesus' identification with the physically poor and reads simply "Blessed are the poor."

Our debt to this type of biblical scholarship is immense, and we can never go back to a pre-critical period. One of the results of it, however, was a weakening of trust in the gospels as historical documents. There were those who began to ask whether anything in the New Testament could be believed absolutely, and whether belief in a historical Jesus was even necessary. A German scholar, Rudolf Bultmann, argued that it is not the historical Jesus but the "Christ of faith" preached to us by the church who makes us new creatures and who is essential for faith. He contended that we need not support our faith with the myths used by ancient people, such as the miracle and resurrection stories. He said the New Testament can and indeed should be "demythologized" or stripped of its supernatural elements and its basic truths re-emphasized.

Despite all that Bultmann has taught us about the New Testament, his theology has probably had its day. Many of Bultmann's own disciples began to point out that in fact there is a fairly substantial body of New Testament material which is not seriously in question. Certainly, an extraordinarily remarkable man, Jesus of Nazareth, lived in Palestine in the time of Caesar Augustus and Pontius Pilate. He undertook a public ministry about the year A.D. 30. He spoke of God as "Father," and announced the coming of God's Kingdom (God's Rule). He commanded his hearers to love one another. He had a reputation for healing the sick. He associated with the poor and the outcasts of society, became alienated from the religious and political authorities, and was executed as an enemy of the state. His followers founded a community and movement on the basis of the proclamation that he had risen from the dead.

Most Christians, responding to the gospel story with the ears of faith will affirm more, especially the resurrection itself. As for the words and teaching of Jesus, there is a widespread view among many New Testament scholars that we have underestimated the proven ability of ancient peoples to preserve vast bodies of oral tradition with great accuracy. In addition, we have failed to account for the sheer originality and incomparable beauty of much New Testament material which carries the stamp of a single great mind. If the vivid parables and pithy sayings of Jesus recorded in the gospels are merely the product of members of the early church, then we must hypothesize the existence of some other very remarkable person or persons who invented them and then ascribed them fictionally to Jesus. This is surely absurd.

One reason for the revival of interest in the historical Jesus has probably been the worsening of living conditions for many people in many parts of the globe, together with the

THAT JESUS IS THE CHRIST AND THAT YOU MAY HAVE LIFE THROUGH HIS NAME THESE ARE RECORDED SO THAT YOU MAY BELIEVE

maturation of their own Christian faith. Christians living in places where people are desperately poor, in situations of blatant political and economic injustice, know the urgency to act now, and have felt the need of a clear, strong model for their action. An idea-principle will not do. They are turning back for another look at the historical Jesus, and insisting that the "Christ of faith" and the historical Jesus are one. "He is who he was."[3]

In addition, they are anything but enamoured with the western forms of civilization, including the church we have passed on to them. By going back to the Jesus of the gospels they have a base from which to judge our much overlaid western Christianity, a Christianity encrusted with almost 2,000 years of our theology, ritual, and miscellaneous cultural trappings. A Brazilian theologian Leonardo Boff says,

"If we identify Jesus with the teaching of the church, then we lose every critical element and the possibility of legitimate protest... From what point of departure can we maintain a critical attitude toward the church if Christ, as Bultmann says, is created by the faith of that same church.... Christ is not primarily an idea, a theme for preaching. He was above all a historical being - conditioned, datable."[4]

The search for the historical Jesus is on again.

KNOWING THE PERSON JESUS

Finally, it needs saying that we cannot discover the real Jesus by simply collecting up the facts, even by collecting up the facts with great skill and honesty. Jesus was a person and one does not learn about a person in the same way as one learns about things, a chemical or mathematical formula, a rock or a tree. Facts and analyses are not sufficient. They don't reach the core. The only appropriate way, indeed the only way to find out about a person is to approach him or her sympathetically, openly, responsively, and with Jesus, if we are Christians, in trust that God will guide us in our search.

Jesus himself reaches out to us through the scriptures, and we respond to him as a person or not at all. He is described as one who acted and spoke with authority and we, hearing that authority in the gospels, find ourselves commanded by him. We have to experience the weight and power of his personality and feel that his words and actions make sense in the light of our own experience.

It is also true, of course, that we discover Jesus together as a Christian community and that he must grasp us as a community. I have my interpretations of him and you have yours and together we can correct and augment our understanding. And we are further nourished by the insights of Christians all over the world, and by those who have lived before us. Christianity was never meant to be a private affair, and we in the West have done our faith a serious disservice by trying to make it so. In formulating our belief, as in other aspects of Christian life and service, we need each other.

There is, however, a time when each, alone, must look at Jesus, and what he said and did must ring true for us personally. For in the end, in the solitude of our own soul, we are still left with the question, "Who do you say that I am?"

## CHAPTER TWO

# LIFE FOR THE POOR

"Come to me, all who labour and are heavy laden, and I will give you rest."

*Matt. 11:28*

"The spirit of the Lord is upon me
because he has anointed me to preach good news
to the poor.
He has sent me to proclaim release to the captives
and recovering of sight to the blind,
to set at liberty those who are oppressed,
to proclaim the acceptable year of the Lord."

*Luke 4:18-19*

"He lived on earth very much the same way as blacks are forced to live. He has made their life his own: he has identified himself with them. He is the black Messiah."

*Allan Boesak (South African black theologian)*

Like the poor of Jesus' time, the poor of our time are appropriating him as their own. And it may be that he is "theirs" in ways that he has not been "ours" for a very long time. It may be also that by looking at him from their perspective we can snap him into a truer and more balanced focus. What they are saying is that, above all else, "Jesus was poor," that this is the most central and indisputable fact about the historical Jesus.

If they are right, and if a person can only be known in relationship, then Jesus' relationship to the poor must be the place to begin our search.

It has been said of Jesus that he wasn't very choosy about the company he kept. But perhaps that is precisely what he was: choosy. By all accounts, he deliberately and consciously chose to associate himself with the poor, for, by background, Jesus was not poor. His father was a carpenter and as things were done two thousand years ago in Galilee, the boy Jesus would have divided his day between attendance at the synagogue school and work in Joseph's shop. This means that he was not "one of the illiterate rabble who do not know the law" (John 7:49). He was educated. He knew the ancient Hebrew language, which was not the spoken language of the day, and he had a thorough knowledge of the scriptures. He was probably a skilled and respected tradesman. The carpenters of Galilee were not only responsible for the building and repair of houses and furniture but, equally important in an agricultural community, for the production of farm equipment. Jesus was "middle class" and probably had no real disadvantage in his own society except that of being a Galilean,[1] - "Can any good thing come out of Nazareth" (John 1:46)?

Why, then, did he make this peculiar choice of companions? As the gospel writers tell it, it can only have been out of love, a reckless, extravagant, generous love that ended with his execution. It was what the Bible calls "compassion," but compassion is a poor translation for the original Greek word. In Greek, the word means an overpowering emotion welling up from the depths of the body, a "gut reaction." The gospel writers say again and again that he saw the crowds and the sick and had compassion on them (Mark 1: 41, Matt. 9:36, 14:14, 15:32, 20:34). Even where the word compassion is not expressly used, that is clearly the emotion behind Jesus' words and actions. Consider his comments on the poor widow putting her pennies in the treasury box. Jesus says over and over again to these people, "Don't worry. Don't be afraid. Cheer up" (Mark 5:36, 6:50, Matt. 6:25, 27, 28, 31, 34, 9:2, 22, 10:19, 26, 28, 31, 14:27, Luke 12:32, John 16:33).

To appreciate the depth of Jesus' concern for them, it is worth looking briefly at who these "poor" were.

## THE BENT ONES

Along the African trail came a very old woman, quite literally bent double with a bag of grain on her back. She was walking seven kilometres to the mill, and when we took the bag from her it was leaden, almost impossibly heavy, even for us. Without the load she didn't straighten. She couldn't. She'd been walking this trail all her life and, she told us, she was fifty-one.

One of the Hebrew words for poor carries the meaning of "bent" or "bowed down," and Jesus most certainly had these bent ones in mind when he said "Blessed are the poor." Most of the land in Palestine was owned by rich land-owners and most of the people were landless peasant farmers. They were heavily taxed by Rome and the temple, and were frequently at the mercy of the money-lender. Then there were the day labourers who earned one denarius a day, just enough to eat, and who were often underemployed or unemployed.

Worse off were the beggars, the widows and orphans. Lacking modern welfare and medical schemes, the sick and disabled, if they had no relative to look after them, were forced to beg. Women, if widowed, had no way of earning a living, and they and their children had to rely on relatives or the charity from pious societies and the temple offerings.

The "poor" of Jesus' time would have looked very little different from the average world citizens today. A family usually had one small hut made of clay bricks, with one window and door. They had two meals a day consisting of a little barley bread with cabbage or turnip and onion or garlic. Fuel was limited, so the vegetables would be eaten raw. Except for feasts, they drank water. They wore a short tunic covered by a long loose linen cloak which also served as a not very warm blanket at night.

The *degree* of their poverty is, to our comfort-soaked minds, barely imaginable. This is one picture reflected in the Mishna, a collection of Jewish rabbinical writings from about the second century B.C. to the second century A.D.

A woman is sitting kneading her bread, clothed only in her long hair which falls to her waist. Has she just washed her tunic, or could it be that she doesn't own one? She and her husband may share a cloak (the very poor did) and he is out in the fields working. So in the cold of the early morning she shapes her bread, carefully setting aside a tenth of it as their tithe. Because of her poverty, she is permitted to make her tithe and to recite other prayers and benedictions, even though she is naked. To be poor in this society is no reason for being poor toward God. God's portion is never a matter of "what we can afford."[2]

Like the very poor today, their poverty contrasted sharply with the enormous wealth of the local elite. An aristocratic widow in Jesus' time was, for example, awarded by the courts, a *daily personal allowance* of roughly 250 dollars[3] - a degree of conspicuous consumption rivalling the Mercedes Benz of our Third World.

But poverty then as now is usually not simply a matter of inadequate housing or food or clothing. There is more than one way of being "bent," and we can never talk about "the poor" as though they were "out there." In a remote African village, where food is precious, a woman gives us two eggs as a welcoming gift. We are awed by the richness of her spirit. Beside her we, in our good clothes, feel shamefully poor.

Poverty can be, as it too often is in North America, a spiritual emptiness or meaninglessness, a continual need for excitement (that fix of adrenalin), or the notion that nothing and no one matters beside our own well-being.

Poverty is also the lack of control over our own lives. The South American peasant working the large estate, or the black South African miner living in barracks may be obvious examples. But are we so immune to this form of poverty? How much real control do many of us have over the type of work we do, where we work, our working conditions? How much control do we have over what goes on at the various levels of government? How far can most of us deviate from the accepted pattern of North American living? Are we not perhaps like the pampered house slave of the southern United States plantations who, unlike the field hand, has every comfort, but little real freedom?

Poverty can be the lack of opportunity to develop our abilities, because of economic deprivation, sexism, racism, - again, a condition rife in the Third World, but far from unknown in the First.

Poverty is a lack of respect from other human beings, the feeling of smallness, that we don't matter. It is a form of poverty we at times all experience, but through human history it has been far more prevalent among the economically poor.

Jesus looking at the economically poor of his time probably saw not just the meanness of their possessions, but also the stultifying narrowness of their lives, their lack of control over what happened to them and their lack of status. It was to these people his heart went out, these and the "sinners."


THE SINNERS

The "sinners" included those with unclean or suspect professions: the prostitutes, tax collectors, usurers, gamblers. There was also a  group of professionals morally suspect because they had to deal with women: goldsmiths, launderers, weavers. (Women as a group among the "poor" we shall look at in another chapter.) "Sinners" included all those whose ancestry was not purely Jewish, who didn't pay their tithes to the priest or who didn't or couldn't keep the large number of complicated religious laws. The illiterates who could not study the law were inevitably in this class. As a group, the sinners obviously overlapped with the economically poor.

There was no practical way for the "sinners" to reverse their situation. They could go through an elaborate purification ritual but this cost money and ill-gotten gains (e.g. from prostitution or taxes) could not be used. They would also have to give up their profession. The uneducated could go through a long educational process, but for most people this was unrealistic.

The "sinners" were denied civil and religious rights. They couldn't hold office and were excluded from the synagogue. They were "unclean" and so could not console themselves

THE SPIRIT OF THE LORD IS UPON ME BECAUSE HE HAS ANOINTED ME TO PREACH GOOD NEWS TO THE POOR

that at least they were acceptable in the eyes of God. To be righteous you had to fulfil the law and this they were not able to do. They were wracked with anxiety about the kinds of divine punishment that might befall them, and in the case of the sick and disabled, tormented with guilt over the sins that they or their parents must have committed to cause their misfortune.

Taken as a group, the poor and the sinners were the large majority of the population and it was to them especially Jesus decided he had been sent. He said that he had come to bring them life and bring it in all its fulness.

But *life* in the New Testament doesn't have the smallness of our English word. It carries the idea of salvation, of wholeness, of total spiritual-physical well-being, of life, as Jesus says, "in all its fulness" (John 10:10). He proposed to do this in basically three ways:
- he healed them
- he lived and associated with them on a common daily level.
  You might say, he lived "in solidarity" with them
- he promised them the Kingdom of God.

JESUS THE HEALER

The healing miracles are difficult for many modern  people. They offend our scientific sensibilities, and despite the recent charismatic wave and a general softening toward such unusual physical and psychological phenomena as extrasensory perception and transcendental meditation, we still tend to associate healing miracles with the more extreme sects. The miracle stories, however, won't go away. The gospels are riddled with them, probably because they were what the average person remembered most about Jesus. Nor can they be minimized. The gospel writers and almost certainly Jesus himself saw his work as healing the sick and preaching the good news of the Kingdom. "And he went about all Galilee teaching in the synagogues and preaching the gospel of the Kingdom and healing every disease and infirmity among the people" (Matt. 4:23).

One of the problems may be that it is easy to see how other

people are conditioned but difficult to see how our background may have closed our minds to a whole range of phenomena that people in cultures outside our own, even today, take for granted. The Jews of that time did not make our distinctions between natural and supernatural. The miracles were God's more extraordinary works.

C.S. Lewis once remarked in a sermon that if for modern western people the end of the world appeared with all the trappings of the book of Revelation, - great white throne, lake of fire, "they would continue forever in that lake itself to regard (their) experience as an illusion and find the explanation for it in psychoanalysis and cerebral pathology."[4] There must surely be more things in heaven and earth than we are able to wrap our twentieth century minds around.

Jesus himself seems to have had a great distaste for being known as a wonder-worker, a bedazzler of the crowds. He often says "Tell no one" (e.g. Matthew 8:4, Mark 7:36). Probably the second temptation has to do with this: "Throw yourself down from the temple," Satan says. He refuses.

The healing miracles were clearly acts of compassion, and Jesus seems to have regarded them as signs that the Kingdom of God had arrived: "If it is by the Spirit of God that I cast out demons then the Kingdom of God has come upon you" (Matt. 12:28).

He is also quite explicit about how they were done. He says "Your faith has made you well (Mark 10:52, Matt. 9:22, 29, Luke 8:48, 17:19): not any psychic powers, not himself and not even explicitly God, but "faith." Faith here can only mean the conviction that what is good and right can happen, will happen. It is almost identical with hope and is the opposite of fatalism, the everyday deadliness of "You can't change the world."

The real miracle was not so much that Jesus healed people as that in their hopeless situation he was able to create this conviction in them. It released in them a power that was able to change impossible circumstances. They caught it from him and they could only have done so because he lived among them.

JESUS THE PARTY GOER

In the gospels, Jesus is no sympathizer who espoused the cause of the poor and then went home to the Palestinian equivalent of a well-carpeted house in the suburbs. He spent time with them, probably most of his time. Read through the gospels with an eye to whom he was with. You'll find that he was sometimes with his disciples, occasionally with a member of the ruling class, but usually with the crowds, the sick, women, "sinners." It's difficult at our distance in time to grasp the implications of this. Then it was a scandal. Jesus' critics asked the disciples, "Why do you eat and drink with tax collectors and sinners" (Luke 5:30)? Eating together has always been a sign of more than feeding. It is a sign of friendship. In the scriptures, Jesus invited people for meals (Mark 2:15) and was invited for meals (Luke 7:36) and even on occasion invited himself for meals (Luke 19:5). More often than not, the meals were "with those people, you know." What his critics were objecting to was not just the fact that he was eating with them, but was enjoying himself. They called him a glutton and a drunkard (Matt. 11:19).

The verbs that are used indicate that these meals were not casual "drop in and pull up a chair" affairs, although no doubt those occurred too. They were parties. The guests reclined at the table as they would at a dinner party (Mark 2:15, Matt. 9:10, Luke 5:29). That's a small fact, but it should put a crack in the dull pietistic shell in which we've often encased Jesus. Jesus was a party goer. He liked to eat and drink, and there can be little doubt that he could tell a good story.

Jesus was, however, regarded as a rabbi, sometimes as a prophet, and what he must have been shouting by his presence there was not only, "I approve of you" but "God approves of you." God forgives you (and notice incidentally that he says "Your sins are forgiven," "Your faith has saved you"). He told them to call God "Abba," the Aramaic equivalent of Daddy. And for people who were considered to be religiously beyond the pale, many of whom were excluded from the synagogue, this must have been very good news.

Jesus actually defended them against the religious leaders. The law was made for people and not people for the law. He knew the scriptures, was clever, and even by his enemies acknowledged as fearless (Matt. 22:16). He could argue with them successfully, - as it happened, too successfully: "No one was able to answer him a word, nor from that day did any one dare to ask him any more questions" (Matt. 22:46).

In a small South African town where we had stopped for petrol, our "coloured" adopted son took a careful, calculated-to-miss swipe at a passing white boy who had been staring at him. As we made the appropriate parental noises we happened to look up and over at the black garage attendants. Their faces were beaming with pure, unadulterated joy.

Reading through the gospels you can sometimes catch this gleam of delight in the eyes of the crowd. Jesus was doing for them what they couldn't or wouldn't do for themselves. It had its consequences, of course, and Jesus, who cautioned his would-be-followers to count the cost before they attached themselves to him, must have certainly done so himself. Was he a fool? Well maybe, but what he did in first century Palestine was create joy. A Peruvian Christian, Gustavo Gutierrez, speaks of joy as having a subversive quality. It weakens the grip of terror and creates life where before there was only death.[5]

JESUS AND THE KINGDOM

Finally, what Jesus did was to promise them the Kingdom of God. He gave them the assurance that God's Kingdom was being established on earth and provided a vision of them, the lame, the lepers, the prostitutes and criminals marching into it ahead of the respectable synagogue goers (Matt. 21:31).

Like the miracles, the Kingdom is for many of us, troublesome. The word isn't in our everyday vocabulary and yet since childhood we have chanted "Thy Kingdom come...for thine is the Kingdom." We know it probably has some connection with God ruling our hearts, possibly with the end of the world and/or with heaven. Beyond that, it drifts into unreality.

It's troublesome for biblical scholars, too, and possibly, in some ways, for the gospel writers themselves. Matthew, for example, in chapter 24 lumps together sayings about the Kingdom, the second coming of Christ and the fall of Jerusalem. Sorting out the separate threads is difficult. But like the healing miracles, it cannot honestly be glossed over. According to Jesus, this is what he was all about: "I must preach the good news of the Kingdom of God to the other cities also; for I was sent for this purpose" (Luke 4:43). Everything else about Jesus is only an elaboration on this.

We can probably only begin to understand his words against his own background as a Jew and against the times in which he was living.

Throughout the Old Testament, the prophets had a dream of God's Kingdom finally coming on earth. Now is a time of suffering, when evil has the upper hand. Then "He shall not judge by what his eyes see or decide by what his ears hear; but with righteousness he shall judge the poor, and decide with equity for the meek of the earth" (Isaiah 11:3-4).

The Jews as a nation looked forward to a time when "of peace there will be no end" (Isaiah 9:7). And it was most definitely going to happen in history. "Your Kingdom come" means the same as "your will be done on earth." (Matthew, out of reverence for the word God usually said Kingdom of Heaven rather than Kingdom of God.) Jesus' Jewish listeners would have known very well that he was talking about a total reordering of this world.

We shall return to the political activity of first century Palestine and Jesus' involvement in a later chapter. It is only necessary to note here that those were times of unusual political upheaval. There was intense guerrilla warfare against the Romans, and many people were expecting God to intervene in their affairs momentarily. What Jesus was saying to them was that God was intervening, but not in the way they had expected.

It's easy for us now to lose sight of the fact that Jesus was very much a man of his own time speaking to his own time. Like all prophets, his message was specific. He was dealing with the problems of his own people and, reading the signs of

the times, what he saw was a society shaky within and oppressed from without. He saw a society plunging toward an
unprecedented catastrophe. (As happened in A.D. 70 with
the massacre and destruction of Jerusalem and again in A.D.
135 when the Jews were finally sent into exile. Until 1948, it
was the effective end of the Jewish nation state.)

What Jesus was preaching with a passion was that the Jews
should turn off this suicidal course now. "Unless you change
you will all be destroyed" (Luke 13:3, 5). "Repent!" (in the
plural). "Turn around." He was saying that this time was
one of opportunity. It was an opportunity for something
totally new to happen in human history. For the first time
they could build together a nation based not on self-interest,
but on co-operation, sharing, compassion. Jesus' appeal was
to all his fellow Jews, but to the poor he gave the assurance
that in this society they would have full and equal citizenship.
That is not to say they would have a guaranteed passport;
they would have to do justice and love mercy like anyone else.
But there they would have all their physical needs met and
would be given their full dignity as human persons.

When the Kingdom would come is, even in the gospels,
problematic. There can be little doubt that Jesus hoped it
would come fully then. He and his disciples were going
throughout the towns of Palestine with great urgency telling
the people to become part of the Kingdom, to help bring it in
in all its glory, then.

What is also clear is that Jesus believed that the Kingdom
had already arrived. It had irreversibly dawned with him,
with his presence in the world. ("If it is by the Spirit of God I
cast out demons, then the Kingdom of God has come upon
you" Matt. 12:28.) When it would be completed no one but
God knew. ("Watch therefore for you know neither the day
nor the hour" Matt. 24:42, 25:13.) Nevertheless, it is all the
time growing and cannot be uprooted. ("The Kingdom of
God is like a grain of mustard seed" Luke 13:19.)

There is a tension in the gospels, a tension still very much
present in the Church today, about what God does and what
we do to bring in this Kingdom. According to Jesus, the
Kingdom was a gift of God ("Do not fear little flock, it is

your Father's pleasure to give you the Kingdom'' Luke 12:32), but at the same time he was pleading with his people to help establish it on earth.

Although we view it from a different time frame, we can still affirm that the Kingdom has come with Jesus, that in spite of the many appearances to the contrary, it is growing in our midst, and that in God's time it will be completed. The Church's task, however, is not merely to wait. The creation of the Kingdom is God's work, but it is also ours.

The people of his day didn't respond to the challenge and we can now only speculate what would have happened if they had. But for the poor it meant that God had seen their suffering and had come to help them. It gave them reason for hope.

And, says an Indian Christian Sebastian Kappen, "Hope is not just one virtue among others, like chastity or patience, which one may fail to practise and yet live. It is the very climate of the human spirit, the air it breathes in order to live. To lose hope is to die."[6]

What Jesus gave them was life.

## CHAPTER THREE

# JESUS, THE POOR AND US

"Take away from me the noise of your songs;
To the melody of your harps I will not listen.
But let justice roll down like waters,
And righteousness like a mighty stream."

*Amos 5: 23, 24*

"Take heed and beware of all covetousness; for a
man's life
does not consist in the abundance of his possessions."

*Luke 12:15*

"Nobody knows the trouble I've seen
Nobody knows but Jesus."

*Negro Spiritual*

The poor today like the poor of his time identify with Jesus as a pushed around little man who lived as one of them. The People's Mass of the Nicaraguans says:

"You are the God of the poor
The human and humble God
The God that sweats in the street
The God of the worn and leathery face.
That is why we speak to you."[1]

They identify with him because he suffered. A black American, James Cone writes, "The Risen Lord's identification with the suffering poor today is just as real as was his presence with the outcasts in first century Palestine...like yesterday, today he also takes the pain of the poor upon himself and bears it for them."[2]

They identify with him because he died. An El Salvadorian, Jon Sobrino, after describing the blood bath in which his country lives, says, "If he is 'the poor' it is because he ended as he ended, crucified, dead." He adds, "Who are the poor? Those who die."[3]

They are insisting that Jesus today has a face and that is the face of the poor. Jesus is the political prisoner in a Korean jail. He is the child on the streets of Bombay. For Canadians he must also be:

- the new Vietnamese immigrant struggling to learn English
- the native Indian and Inuit fighting for land rights
- the elderly person living on an old-age pension
- the disabled, the retarded
- the person with the least status in the community around us and in our own immediate environment.

But what specifically is Jesus doing for the world's poor? To assume that God's Spirit is working only through Christians would, of course, be worse than arrogant. Wherever the hungry are being fed, and prisoners freed, God is at work building the Kingdom. However, among those who call him "Lord," Jesus is doing now what he did then.

HE HEALS THEM

From the Nyadiri Methodist Hospital in Zimbabwe, a young doctor writes:

The church has been an integral part of the national development. Many of the country's leaders were educated at mission schools. The missions still provide essential education and health services. The community at Nyadiri Methodist Mission runs a primary and secondary school, a nurses' training school, a teachers' training college, and the hospital. The hospital is a rambling red brick building with a galvanized roof. The wards will hold two hundred beds.

In an average month we have 190 in-patients, 3,900 out-patients, 120 deliveries, and eight deaths. The mission also runs an orphanage and six outlying clinics. Fortunately, we are three physicians here...[4]

The Church has laid the foundations for medical care and education in much of the Third World and still continues in many areas to provide the only such facilities available. Unfortunately, though, the history and reputation of missions is a very stained garment. The Church went into the Third World hand in hand with the colonizers, and for all their fancy rhetoric about "civilizing the natives," the colonizers were there for one purpose: to exploit the resources of those countries. Because they had the superior weaponry, they succeeded. The involvement of missionaries is blatantly evident in the words of the famous African explorer-missionary, David Livingstone, to a gathering at Cambridge University: "I go back to Africa to make an open path for commerce and Christianity."[5] The exploitation goes on today under the guise of more sophisticated corporations, rather than direct colonial rule, and although the Church may object loudly, its earlier associations are remembered.

Nevertheless, the fact remains that with or without the Church's connivance, colonization would have proceeded, and the Church, through its educational and medical institutions has helped many of the peoples of Africa and Asia to cope with the onslaught of the western world. And ironically, with the twists of time (or is it the scheming of the Holy Spirit), many of the Church's institutions and practices have been changed locally in ways which would have surprised and dismayed the original missionaries. Consider, for example, the Zionists.

Across the hills of southern Africa at night, you hear the drums of the Zionists' healing services. The Zionists are one of many African independent churches, or, as they prefer to be called, indigenous churches. They use the ancient rituals and remedies of African traditional healing and call on the name of Jesus for their impressive spiritual/physical/psychic cures. They are suspect by the more established denominations and are the fastest growing Christian communities in Africa today.

# HE COMFORTS THEM

The rain seeped through the thatch, making small craters in the dirt floor on which we sat. The service had been going on for two and a half hours, liberally interspersed with spontaneous prayers which rose and fell like songs, and spontaneous songs in four-part harmony. The preacher, an "untrained" evangelist, spoke with his Bible open before him. Tears rolled down his cheeks. He was talking about "Jesu Kreste." To reach Mphokojoane, you must walk for several hours along narrow mountain ridges high above the Orange River and you will not find it on any but the local maps. When we asked when the service would begin they replied, "When all the villagers are here."

The Marxists have a lot to say, some of it with justification, about religion being the opium of the people, an other-worldly drug that keeps them from making the necessary changes in their present situation.

People can, however, be trapped in conditions where there is little or no room for change. And if in those circumstances Jesus gives them a conviction of their dignity and self worth, together with the belief that he himself will be waiting for them "on the other side of Jordan," then he is surely meeting a real need. And if, though their scope for action is limited, they are able to give comfort and support to their families and communities, this is no mean thing either. It's true that without hope we die. Only out of hope comes action.

## HE PROMISES THEM THE KINGDOM OF GOD
## AND CHALLENGES THEM TO STRUGGLE FOR IT NOW

Among Third World Christians, there is a new emphasis on what South American Christians have called "praxis." It calls for doing the gospel, doing justice, even when it may be dangerous. Praxis is taking as many forms as the situations and people involved. It may mean teaching illiterate peasants, or setting up a communal fish farm; it may mean joining the government forces in Nicaragua or the guerrillas in South Africa. It is first of all an involvement in a concrete situation based on the certain belief that Jesus wills the liberation and

well being of all his people. All these advocates of praxis have a common emphasis:
- reading the signs of the time: being politically and economically informed so the real causes of inequality and oppression can be discerned
- working out consistently humane and compassionate solutions to problems: a reform that is not compassionate is no reform
- communitarianism: working together with other Christians who share their goals, aware that along the way they may encounter quite unexpected travelling companions
- constructing new models for society and not just patching up old ones: improvements in agriculture are not relevant if the basic issue of land ownership and control has not been dealt with
- commitment: unconditional involvement in the struggle, putting your hand to the plough and not looking back.

That may give you the idea, but it doesn't give you the tone. In places where these Christians are facing genuine hardship and physical danger, there is often a verve and vitality and a solidity of faith that we may very well envy. Steve Biko, for example, a Christian and a black consciousness leader heavily involved in community development, died while being held by the South African security police. He wrote these words:

"A struggle without casualties is no struggle...We have set out on a quest for true humanity, and somewhere on the distant horizon we can see the glittering prize. Let us march forth with courage and determination drawing strength from our common plight and our brotherhood. In time we shall be in a position to bestow upon South Africa the greatest gift possible - a more human face."[6]

He had no doubts about the final outcome of the struggle.

WHAT ABOUT US?

It only remains, then, to slot ourselves into the picture. How do we relate to the poor in our own society, and particularly to the poor in that amorphous mass, the Third World? How do we reflect Jesus' compassion in our attitudes and actions toward them? Jesus had the advantage of seeing the poor daily as he walked the villages of Palestine. They were omnipresent. For us more often than not, they are abstractions on our television screen or lists of statistics in our newspapers, and for us to relate to them requires a far greater effort of imagination. The poor in Canada we tend to make as invisible as possible (witness, for example, the difficulty of establishing homes for battered women in residential communities), and some of us may have to scuff the dust a little to see them.

A farmer teaching part time tells this joke in the staff room:
Question: "What would you do with a million dollars?" Farmer: "I'd farm until it ran out." Says a fellow teacher blankly, "I don't get it."

The congregation is coming out of a small white church in a northern Ontario farming community. The church looks down over the lake and forests and is wrapped in a peace and beauty which makes city dwellers wistful. But someone starts talking about a recent suicide and another one about the lack of rain and the mood abruptly changes. A farmer near us shrugs. "It's frustration. It doesn't matter how hard you work or how good your crops are, you never make anything. A farmer just outside Toronto makes a couple of dollars on a hog. Here the transportation costs eat up the profit. One of those government fellows told me I'd be better off on welfare. He says we can buy our food cheaper from Argentina."

A woman from the Holland Marsh, some of the best market garden land in Canada, tells us theirs is the only family farm in her immediate area. The rest are operated by large agribusinesses.

All the pieces are there, but we seldom fit them together. The Canadian government's recent Brinkman Report does. Most of the farms and most of the farmland in Canada are still run on a small scale by families, but at least half of their income is being earned in jobs outside the farm. They grow our food, but they support themselves with earnings from other jobs.[7] They are subsidizing the rest of us. But as incomes fall and costs rise, more small farms are being forced to sell out. The loss in human skill, resourcefulness and dignity, and control over the land is staggering. This lost control over the land has a neater modern name. It's called "the Third World." The specialization of food crops for export and large scale imports of basic food stuffs is a familiar Third World pattern, and is happening increasingly in Canada.

A block away from the carefully mowed suburban lawns is a series of high-rise apartments. The grounds are littered with rubbish and the grass uncut. A tenant, a young divorced woman with two children says the hardest thing to get used to in moving there was the way her kids are treated. "Everyone assumes a kid is noisy and destructive."

Compared with the poor of Jesus' time and the poor of our globe today, she's wealthy. She isn't physically bent (but she is up at 6:30 to prepare supper, then breakfast, and get the kids ready for school. By 8:00 at night and too often during the day she's dead bone weary). She has political and legal rights (but when she complained about preferential treatment in parking spaces, her car tires were anonymously slashed). She has a strong sense of self worth and personal dignity (but she's continually embarrassed by the propositions of married men at her office). She isn't destitute. As an office worker she earns enough. (But of the annual office dinner dance which costs twenty dollars, she says "I just don't have that kind of money to spend on myself.")

If she were on welfare, however, she would receive a total of $6,592 in the Toronto area (1982) and would have to move across to the public housing block, which is decorated with angry obscenities and entered through knots of angry looking teenagers. If she had to work as a waitress for minimum wage she would be classed by the government as "the working poor" and fall below the poverty line in every Canadian province except Quebec.[8]

We could provide a blank box here with the caption "Supply your own examples." They are unlimited.

Justice and compassion can only dictate a fairer distribution of income, a wiser use of our resources, particularly human resources, and adequate support systems, both personal and governmental. But perhaps there is also a legitimate selfish consideration here. We are all part of one community, one nation. If different parts of the body are hurting, eventually we'll feel thoroughly miserable. A few farmers forced to sell out may seem to affect us very little, but, says one expert in the field, "When industry takes over agriculture and has the power to put the price of the land on the product, consumers are going to pay it. At that point half the people in North America won't be able to eat."[9] As women, we may look, briefly, at single mothers and realize that some of us are only one man away from a very skimpy income. But there are in Canada today a large number of women in that situation, and their children, who bear the emotional weight are the next generation of Canadians. If as a nation we are going to be healthy, we must *all* be healthy. The same principle, by extension, applies to our well-being as a world community. "Out there" are 75 percent of the world's poorest people, and whether we like it or realize it, we are intimately bound up in their welfare.

OUR GLOBAL COMMUNITY

How we as individuals are involved in the problem of world poverty is far from self evident. Consider, for example, these two statements, one by E.F. Schumacher, an economist, and one by John Raines in *The Christian Century*. (They are written about Americans but could apply equally well to Canadians.)

"Think of it: one American drawing on resources that would sustain fifty Indians! The earth cannot afford, say 15 percent of its inhabitants - the rich who are using all the marvellous achievements of science and technology - to indulge in a crude, materialistic way of life which ravages the earth. The poor don't do much damage; the modest people don't do much damage...The problem passengers on Space-ship Earth are the first-class passengers and no one else."[10]

"Generally speaking, the takeoff point for 'making it' in America comes only at the $25,000 a year line (or the 1983 equivalent, about $36,000). That line is already beyond 95 percent of us...and it is constantly moving further away under the double pressure of the majority crush below and the escalating concentration of wealth above...Affluent? Comfortable? With the father holding two jobs and/or the mother working, our family will have to cope day after day with turmoil at home, defeat at the super-market and persistent exhaustion. No, there isn't much of a 'mid-dle' in America today. There is a top, and then there are all the rest of us pounding along on the endless stampede, wondering why we're always so tired.''[11]

Can both statements possibly be true? Can so many of us be both ridiculously affluent and struggling to make all the ends meet at the same time? Probably the most basic truth of the matter is that many of us are caught up in a way of life which cannot be sustained in either global terms or in terms of our own economy. It won't work globally because it is rapidly using up the world's limited resources and im-poverishing a large proportion of its people and increasingly, with the pollution of the environment, inflation, and various attendant ills, it is not working at home either.

To cast the average Canadian or American as the knowing villain of the piece would be both unfair and inaccurate. She or he is also tied into an economic system and on a very short leash. The system jolts and so do we.

To say, however, that we're not to blame is very different from saying that we aren't implicated.

We're implicated because Canadian companies purchase cheap raw materials from Third World countries (at prices largely dictated by us) and sell them expensive manufactured goods (at prices dictated by us). As our inflation rate rises, their problems are accentuated a hundred fold. Ten years ago Ghana could buy a tractor for one ton of cocoa. Now she has to sell five tons for the same tractor![12]

Where investment goes on in the Third World, the type of production is geared almost entirely to the needs of Cana-dians, not the local population, and profits come back to Canada or the United States. That's not to say that invest-ment isn't highly desirable in these capital starved economies, but could investment be done more to our mutual benefit? Is it conceivable that Canadian companies, having trained local personnel, could gradually, after a limited period of profit making, transfer the company control to a local public cor-poration?

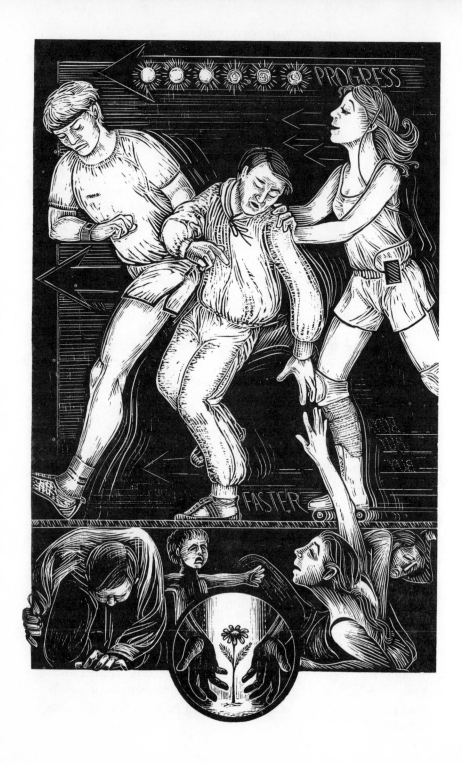

Unfortunately, if such arrangements occur, they will probably have to be initiated by the Third World countries concerned and right now that is not often likely to happen. Many, if not most Third World countries are controlled by elites who are quickly becoming richer and more powerful while the lot of the average citizen deteriorates. It's doubtful whether many of these elites would demand types of development and investment that would benefit the citizens widely and equally. What is most needed in many instances is, first of all, reform or revolution within the country itself, particularly in the ownership of land.

These instances cited by Frances Moore Lappé are not unusual.

"In the Philippines where rice production has almost doubled in the last decade, the population's average consumption of grain has sunk to the lowest in all Asia...

"In Thanjavur, India, for example, new technologies have increased rice yields to three times the national average. But the underpaid landless day labourers who harvest the rice must survive by eating rats that thrive on the mountains of stored surplus rice."[13]

Where farmers don't control their land, their life will never improve. We might ask whether it's necessary for Canadian investors to keep propping up elitist governments. Is it possible for the Canadian government to adopt a strong alternative stance to that of the Americans in situations of obvious oppression, such as El Salvador and Guatemala? Is it at all possible that more economic support could be put behind governments which show evidence of being broadly representative of the people, e.g. Nicaragua, Tanzania, Zimbabwe? Otherwise, with all the good will in the world our development aid and investment will be largely wasted. The raw fact is that "in the thirty years since the development concept was launched, there has been no substantial improvement in the lot of the poor in those nations which have been the recipients of our aid, and with the present workings of the international economic system *there never will be.*"[14]

That's not to say that government and church aid cannot be beneficial. It can, but only if it is carried out with the total involvement and approval of the people who are going to benefit directly. If it is given, it must be a well-thought-out leg up and not a strings attached handout. (Eighty percent of government aid money still has to be spent on Canadian goods and personnel.)[15] What Third World countries need are just economic arrangements, not charity.

All this, of course, puts only a few surface scratches on the world economic problem, but the inescapable fact remains that through imports, exports, investments, and development, Canadians are implicated in the global situation.

But if we are implicated, are we then responsible? Many very sincere church people when faced with the world situation feel vaguely guilty but conclude, in all seriousness, that nothing can be done. They argue that it is naive to think we can influence multinational corporations or the World Bank, to say nothing of the Canadian government. At home we are locked into a society where to function we must have electricity and appliances, a car, and adequate housing, all requiring considerable expenditure; to think we can change the world poverty problem by eating only one meat meal a week, or walking to work, is absurd.

We don't agree. We would suggest that, though our room to manoeuvre is small, we can still take some effective action, and if enough of us do so, who is to say what the final outcome might be? To do nothing is a sin against hope.

There is in North America a rapidly growing movement toward a simpler life-style and global justice, and those involved insist these must go together. If we become involved in global justice issues without changing our own consumer patterns, no one will take us seriously. But to simplify our life-style alone is also not enough. In the longer term, it may affect the world's poor. In the shorter run, factors like trade agreements and capital investment will have the most impact.

THE SIMPLER LIFE

We follow a Lord who lived simply, chose to ride into Jerusalem on a donkey, who told us to "consider the lilies of the field," and made fun of elegantly dressed people. He knew God is difficult to reach through the clutter. So are the poor.

What many people today are saying is that the plight of the world's poor, when taken seriously, impinges on most aspects of our lives:
- on the way we eat (Do we really need grain-fed beef that badly if feeding cattle uses up a disproportionate amount of the world's grain supply? Twenty-one pounds of grain protein are needed to produce one pound of beef protein)[16]
- on what we drink (Do we need coffee with sugar that much, even if it uses up vast regions of land that could be used for nutritious local crops?)
- on the way we travel (Consider how the extravagant use of fossil fuels in our big cars pushes up the price of oil all over the world)
- on the way we spend our money and the hundred small decisions we make daily about what we buy and what we use.

We have appended a check-list of life-style suggestions, but for every person the choices have to be different, made out of our continual response to our own situation and to God within us.

It's important to realize at the outset that to cut back on our living standards deliberately is to go directly against the whole push of our consumer society. And so, as Doris Longacre says in *Living More With Less,* "If you want to buck traffic, first organize a convoy. To nonconform freely we must strengthen each other."[17] We badly need the support and challenge of family and small groups of like-minded people. We are made to live in communities, and effective change usually includes a group or community. Conscious of this, one family writes, "We try to be consistent, and this essentially means seeking to avoid waste, to set low standards of consumption, to accent the human and personal in our lives, to share resources and to pursue all of this *within the context of community...*Thus the focus in organizing our own lives has tended to be expressed in development of neighbourhood gardens, food co-ops and the like."[18] We build the Kingdom more effectively together.

What people involved in life-style change are also saying is that it does have personal benefits, that to simplify is exhilarating, that the less you need the freer you become, that only free people can laugh at the accepted norms and make choices. It is not a matter of having nothing, but of needing little and so being content. And perhaps that in itself needs emphasizing.

For a long time, people from Hans Selye to Leonard Cohen have been telling us that the rat race is for rats; ecologists and economists have been pointing out that the planet cannot long support our way of living, not to mention extending it to the rest of the world; and thin, sad-eyed children have stared out at us from overseas aid advertisements. Now maybe it's time to say that those hundred small and large decisions to live with less also add up to a richer, not a poorer way of life, and cumulatively, for us as well as for the poor, to a way of life rather than a way of death. Of such is the Kingdom of the future.

GLOBAL JUSTICE

Eduardo is a Guatemalan refugee. As he sits eating with us he points to a basket of bananas on the table. "You don't see the connection between those bananas and our poverty," he says. "My people get fifty cents a day for growing bananas. They can't buy enough food for their family, but Del Monte makes big profits and you pay forty-nine cents a pound for them in Dominion." He doesn't add, "You're living on our backs," because he's too polite.

Since then we've seldom bought bananas, but we're also aware that this has done nothing to change the *present* situation in Guatemala. Eduardo's land would be better used growing food for his family rather than bananas for export. The fact is that if we are to alleviate injustice of this kind we have to change the structures and institutions which are perpetuating it. It means supporting reform within Guatemala itself and questioning the global economic arrangements that make this type of exploitation possible. There is no other way.

World economics and politics often look intimidatingly

large and remote, and most of us would prefer to leave them to someone else. Our church leaders do issue statements on international affairs, make representation to the annual meetings of corporations, have meetings with management and encourage government policy changes. Through our mission givings they direct carefully chosen and well monitored development projects throughout the world.

But some individual churches have Amnesty International groups and are sponsoring refugee families. That's involvement in global justice. Or when a group or individual organizes a protest against a badly managed local public transport system, that's also involvement in global justice.

Making dents in present political-economic policies is, according to those who do it, an acquired skill. You learn by doing. We are all at times angry or annoyed by decisions our governments make. But if, for example, we are unhappy about the federal government's policy regarding Central America, how can we react?

One woman in our congregation suggests having the numbers of the local, provincial, and federal representatives by the phone and giving them or their office a quick call whenever we wish to register our approval or disapproval of an issue. Lois Wilson, former Moderator of The United Church of Canada, suggests many cups of coffee with government representatives, getting to know them personally and making use of the old expedient of letter writing. In fact not many people do.

People involved in social change, however, agree that a well informed and committed group is almost always more successful than individuals. The Nestlé Boycott and the churches' campaigns to have Canadian banks stop loans to South Africa and Chile are evidence of this. As for government, it still has to take note of public opinion, and the more numerous the "public" the more effective the protest. But it is also possible that more of us than we imagine have a talent for politics, even for active participation in political parties, for the long-term development of policies, and for holding political office.

A good, small-scale model for international action is

Bridgehead in Toronto. Four people have started a company that imports tea from Sri Lanka and coffee from Tanzania and Nicaragua. The profits directly benefit the farmers who produce the tea and coffee and not large international companies. A number of churches provide outlets for Bridgehead products.

On a large scale, Amnesty International is probably our best example. It works to free or better the conditions of prisoners of conscience mainly through letter writing. It has over 350,000 members in over 150 countries and is surprisingly effective. "One wishes," comments James Finnerty in *World Citizen,* "that there were an Ecology International with the scope and sophistication of Amnesty International or a Peace International or an Economic Justice International."[19] Is there any reason why there shouldn't be?

We have included in the appendix a list of general guidelines for change. What you do, though, will depend on the injustices and the issues you feel angry and disturbed about. It may be that the most underused resources in the problem of global justice are personal emotions and our human brains.

We seem to have strayed a long way from the poor of Jesus' time, but maybe not so far. Is the landless peasant of Palestine so different from the landless peasant of north-east Brazil? Is the woman who was "a sinner from the city," who was given a frosty reception at Simon's party so different from the street woman in a large Canadian city who on a bad night sleeps in the entrance to the art gallery because there are no overnight facilities for women? And if we want to call Jesus "Lord" can our response to them be any different than his?

It seems appropriate, then, to give Jesus the last word:

> "I was hungry and you fed me
> I was thirsty and you gave me drink
> I was a stranger and you took me in
> Naked and you clothed me
> In prison and you visited me...
> Whatever you did to one of the least of these
> You did to me."

*Matthew 25:35-4*

## CHAPTER FOUR

# LIFE FOR WOMEN

"They marvelled that he was talking to a woman."

*John 4:27*

"She turned around and saw Jesus standing, but she did not know that it was Jesus. Jesus said to her, 'Woman, why are you weeping? Whom do you seek?' Supposing him to be the gardener she said to him, 'Sir, if you have carried him away, tell me where you have laid him and I will take him away.' Jesus said to her, 'Mary.' "

*John 20: 14-16*

"Have you heard the joke about the astronaut who saw God?" It was the first all women's meeting in that particular African university and the posters announcing it had been covered with angry male graffiti.

"Well," the speaker went on, "an American astronaut returning to earth frantically radioed down that he had just seen God. But no sooner had the stunned technicians at the other end received his message than they lost radio contact. The news went out over the air waves and the world waited with held breath while the space craft landed and the astronaut was put through his de-spacing procedures. When he was finally ready for questioning the media mobbed him.

"God! What was he like?"

The reply came back. "She's black!"

As the punch line took, wide delighted smiles lit the faces of the women in the room. They understood, perfectly.

Poor because they often lack the necessities of life, and poor because of their second class status, Third World women are accustomed to seeing themselves as very far from God-like. Second class status, however, is not confined to Third World women, and to the extent that women in the rest of the world are thought of as inferior and so lack respect, they too are "poor." To the extent that they have less control over their lives than the men around them and less opportunity to develop their abilities, they are also "poor," though their concrete problems may be very different. There is the isolation and mind-destroying boredom of the young North American housewife and mother, the highlight of whose week may be a trip to the local shopping mall. But this is a very different type of oppression from that of the black woman working in a white South African kitchen, forcibly separated from her husband and children and paid a subsistence wage.

For Third World women, their liberation as women has to be tied into  total economic liberation of their people. For women who fight each day for the bare necessities of life or whose young people are being jailed, tortured or who have "disappeared," a separate struggle for personal status is a useless frill. They have the formidable task of struggling alongside their men for the broad well-being of their people and at the same time insisting that their equality as women be an integral part of that well-being. It is being done in many parts of the world today.[1]

The fact that they have different problems, however, doesn't mean that women throughout the world can't give each other mutual understanding and support and recognize that traditionally and currently they do share certain disadvantages.

Rosemary Reuther, an American theologian, lists these as:
- dependency - having to depend on a man for physical support and often for legal and physical protection
- secondary existence - being thought of as inferior or subordinate to men and taking their status and often their sense of identity from the men to whom they are attached, usually father or husband

- domestic labour - being largely limited to work within the home, and therefore, because they have lacked training and opportunity, exhibiting a *de facto* inferiority in many areas ("Where are the female Mozarts, Kierkegaards and Einsteins?")
- sexual exploitation - being used as a sex object
- being defined mainly by their child bearing and child rearing function, and so being valued mainly as a mother and not simply as a human being.[2]

In recognizing these disadvantages, women can also take the hands of their sisters down through history. The women of Jesus' time were "poor" in precisely these ways also. And how Jesus related to them and what he did for them is the main subject matter of this chapter.

•

During the last ten years, Christian feminists (not always women) have been looking at the Bible from a female perspective, focusing particular attention on Jesus. What did he think of women? How did he treat them? What they have discovered, quite incredibly, considering the times in which he lived, is that in the gospels, there is not a single sexist statement or story attributed to Jesus. That's to state the matter negatively. Positively, he healed men and women equally, was friends with women, defended them, broke taboos on their behalf and made them his followers. None of this may sound very startling to twentieth century ears, but from within his society it was almost unthinkable. His words and actions can only be appreciated against the background of first century Palestinian society.

As a preliminary to a discussion of this society, however, we need at least two historical footnotes.

The men of first century Palestine were not unusual among peoples of that time in their treatment of women. The secondary status of women was, with some fluctuations, a generalized condition throughout the ancient world, as it continues to be in many parts of the world today.

Then there is always the serious danger of emotional distortion in looking at the lives of our sisters in the past. We may know what they did, the gritty details of their daily lives, but we don't know how they felt. They may have, and probably did get much satisfaction and fulfillment in situations that we would find demeaning. Undoubtedly women in that society had an honoured place in the home and were regarded as more than "just housewives." Within the family they helped perpetuate the sacred traditions of their people.

Nevertheless, it remains true that they lived in a heavily male-dominated society, a patriarchal society where the male was the "normative Jew" for religious observances,[3] and that, with some notable exceptions, the writing we have from that time about women is overwhelmingly negative.

The great Rabbi Akiba (c. A.D. 40-135) is representative of the exceptions. His attitude to women was consistently gentle and admiring. To the question "What is wealth?" he replies, "A wife who is comely in her deeds." He defended their rights in matters which today may seem insignificant but then were revolutionary. For example, "He conceded that a married working woman should turn over her wages to her husband. But he ruled that if she earned more than he spent on her maintenance the difference belonged to her."[4]

Far more typical of the times are statements and attitudes such as those of Paul ("the head of a woman is her husband... a man...is the image and glory of God; but woman is the glory of man" I Cor. 11:3, 7), or the Rabbi Eliezer, "If any man gives his daughter a knowledge of law it is as though he taught her lechery" (*Mishnah,* Sotah, 3, 4), or the historian Josephus, "The woman, says the law, is in all things inferior to the man" (*Against Apion* 11.201).

In Jesus' society, women were legally children. They belonged to a "master", either a husband, father or brother, and were totally dependent on them. They were a man's property and in the commandment against covetousness rank between a neighbour's house and his manservant.

Only the men had full membership in the religious community. Women, children and slaves were not obliged to recite the morning or mealtime prayers and in his prayers the Jew daily recited, "Praised be God that he has not created me a gentile: praised be God that he has not created me a woman: praised be God that he has not created me an ignorant man" (Tosephta Berakoth 7, 8).[5] Women didn't count in the quorum necessary to hold a religious service and were restricted to the women's court of the temple. They were not allowed to take part in the service and were not allowed to learn the scriptures.

Their general situation can be summed up in a rabbinical saying of the time: "At the birth of a boy all are joyful, but at the birth of a girl all are sad" (Talmud bNiddah 31b).[6] And it is against this background that Jesus' stance leaps out at us. Almost equally startling is the fact that this very negative attitude to women did not filter through the message of the gospel writers. It is further evidence that Jesus' regard for women must have been one of the indisputable emphases of his ministry. If by the term "feminist" we mean someone who actively promotes the full equality of men and women, even when it contravenes the accepted customs of their society, then Jesus was surely a feminist. But how specifically did Jesus bring life to the women he encountered?

HE TALKED WITH THEM

Note first that Jesus was a rabbi and he talked to women in public. One scripture scholar, Peter Ketter, says, "A rabbi regarded it as beneath his dignity, as indeed positively disreputable, to speak to a woman in public." The wise men of Jesus' day said, "Who speaks much with a woman draws down misfortune on himself, neglects the words of the law and finally earns hell" (Mishnah Aboth 1, 5).[7] Jesus here was crashing through the mores of his society.

There are a number of recorded conversations between Jesus and women in the gospels, but take as a sample his discussion with the Samaritan woman at Jacob's well (John 4:5f). His talking to her would have been disreputable on three accounts:
- a Jew would not talk to a Samaritan
- a man would not speak to a woman in public and certainly not if he were a rabbi
- she had a highly suspect style of life, five husbands, and she was not married to the man with whom she was living.

The woman herself was surprised when Jesus spoke to her. "How is it you, a Jew, ask a drink of me, a woman of Samaria?" It's clear from what follows in the story that his speaking to a woman was even more unusual than his speaking to a Samaritan. When the disciples return they are "surprised to see him speaking to a woman, though none of them asked 'What do you want from her? Why are you talking to her?' " Look at the content of their discussion. This isn't casual chit-chat; this is a long, serious conversation. (It may reflect the theology of the early church, yet it is remarkable for its time and must be an indication of the actual attitude of Jesus to women.)

After asking for a drink of water, Jesus talks about himself as "the living water." We don't know the woman's tone of voice. She may have been amused or aggressive, but she questions him closely, "Where do you get that water? Are you greater than our father Jacob who gave us this well?"

Later, after a few comments about her husbands - they do not get side-tracked into her sexual relationships - they go on to discuss the proper place and way to worship God. The woman is familiar with the religious issues here and shows her knowledge of the scriptures by talking about the Messiah who is coming "who will show us all things." Jesus then says "I who speak to you am he." It is one of the very few places in the gospels where Jesus explicitly reveals himself as the Messiah and we might well ask, why to this woman? Was it because she was clever, well informed, enthusiastic? Was it because she already saw him as a prophet, or because he knew she would readily respond? She had immediately said, "Give me this special water." She ran to tell her fellow villagers and "many believed because of her testimony." Whatever Jesus' motive was for this disclosure, it was unlikely his choice of people, and particularly of a woman, was accidental. As a footnote you might notice what he says to his disciples when the woman has gone back to the village: "See how the fields are already white for harvest. " He was certainly referring to potential disciples, but could he have been implying that women, being among "the poor," were particularly open to his message?

Another fascinating, but brief conversation is that of Jesus with the Canaanite woman (Matt. 15: 21f, Mark 7:24f).

According to Mark, Jesus is trying to get away from the crowds and a Canaanite woman pushes her way in. She begs him to heal her mad daughter. Matthew says Jesus would not even speak to her. The disciples ask him to get rid of her. She's making a nuisance of herself. Jesus answers, "I was sent only to the lost sheep of the house of Israel."

The woman persists. You can feel her desperation. She has a terribly sick child and nothing to lose. She falls at Jesus' feet and pleads with him. "Let the children be fed first, for it is not right to take the children's bread and throw it to the dogs," he says. Jesus at this point sees himself as sent to the Jews and not to the gentiles. But dogs? Even though biblical scholars have argued that these were house dogs and not street curs, the sentence still stings. We talk glibly about Jesus being human, but can we allow ourselves to think, even momentarily, that he might have had some of the prejudices of his day?

The woman is smart. She doesn't latch on to his prejudice, doesn't argue that she's not a dog. She single-mindedly wants her daughter healed and to make Jesus feel ashamed won't further her purposes. She uses the good debater's trick of taking her opponent's words and turning them to her own advantage, "Yes, Lord, even the dogs eat the crumbs which fall from their master's table."

Jesus is impressed with her, - her determination, her intelligence, her quick response. In Mark, which is the earlier account, he says, "For this saying, you may go your way: the demon has left your daughter." It is the only time in the gospels where Jesus is talked into changing his mind, and a woman does it.

We also speak of Jesus "growing in wisdom" (Luke 2:52). Could it be that here is an encounter in which Jesus grew in his self understanding and began to conceive of his mission as including the gentiles and not only the Jews? What is evident is that he could have been annoyed, threatened, dismissive, but, like the person of stature he was, he responded to her as a person and publicly commended her.

HE DEFENDED THEM

Jesus, however, didn't just break taboos by talking to them; he actively and aggressively defended women.

One of the most poignant examples of this has to be the case of the "woman from the city who was a sinner" (Matt. 26:6f).

Jesus is at a dinner party at Simon the Leper's house and the guests' feet are probably behind them as they stretch out on couches. The woman comes in quietly and begins to wash Jesus' feet with her tears, wipe them with her hair, kiss them, and pour expensive ointment on them. The act is passionate and extravagant, but also self-assertive and deliberate. No one would just walk around with such an expensive item. She had to get it, probably buy it, and then go to a place where she knew she wouldn't be welcome. Simon and the other male guests are appalled. The woman is unclean, and by touching Jesus she makes him unclean. Doesn't Jesus know what kind of woman she is? They don't see what she's doing. They see only a prostitute. Jesus, however, is not embarrassed. He sees a woman who "loves much." He accepts her action with satisfaction, if not pleasure. It is Simon he criticizes. Simon has not even given him water for his feet, but she has washed them with her tears. He sets her up as an example to the men in the room. His remarks to his host are cutting and his praise of the woman is lavish. In John, he says, "She has done a beautiful thing for me," and in Matthew and Mark, he says, "Truly I say to you, wherever the gospel is preached in the whole world what she has done will be told in memory of her."

Of prostitution he says nothing, only "Your sins are forgiven. Your faith has saved you. Go in peace." (And note again it would not have been proper to speak to a woman publicly, especially one of this kind.)

Another story in the same vein is that of the woman taken in adultery (John 8:3-11). The story itself is very familiar, but notice how the religious authorities are cold-bloodedly using the woman. She has been set up to trap Jesus. If Jesus agrees to her stoning he will contravene Roman law, and if he refuses to stone her he will contravene Mosiac law.[8] Probably his reputation for kindness and defense of women is also being tested. Notice the pitiable state of the woman herself. She has been taken "in the act" and dragged before the crowd where they are "making her stand in full view of everybody." But notice here again it is the men Jesus condemns. "He who is without sin among you throw the first stone." The implication is obvious. They, too, have been involved in sexual misconduct and, shamed, they leave the scene. Jesus is kicking hard at the double standard of his day which punished women severely for their misdemeanours, but seldom men, and then only because they had violated the property rights of their neighbour.

You can feel the life flooding back into the woman. She has been saved from a very savage death. And Jesus, though he has passed judgment on the men, does not pass judgment on the woman, or rather, he passes a positive judgment: "Neither do I condemn you. Go and sin no more."[9]

His statements on marriage and divorce, too, which sound to us highly legalistic, were in reality a blatant defense of women. A man could divorce a woman by simply giving her written note to that effect. Divorce was common and could leave women without any means of support. Jesus tightens the divorce laws: "What God has joined together, let no man put asunder," in an attempt to make the woman's position more secure. Even his disciples think that here he's being too demanding: "If such is the case of a man with his wife, it is not expedient to marry." It is interesting and again certainly deliberate that the Hebrew scripture that Jesus quotes regarding marriage is not the "helpmate" passage and is not one which followed the patriarchal arrangements of his own society. Rather he chooses to quote Genesis 2:24: "A man shall leave his father and mother and be joined to his wife and the two shall become one." In his society it was the *woman* who left *her family* and became the possession of the man and his family. What Jesus is emphasizing is a relationship of equality in which both partners have rights and responsibilities.

HE CHOSE THEM AS FOLLOWERS AND FRIENDS

Jesus had women followers and friends. Luke 8:1 says the twelve were with him and also some women. It names a few of them, - Mary Magdalene, Joanna, Susanna and adds, "and many others who provided for them out of their means." The women travelled around with him and learned from him. At a time when women were religiously very limited and were frequently not allowed to leave the household, the situation was quite extraordinary.

Jesus talked to women individually about faith and instructed them in the scriptures. Besides the story of the Samaritan woman, see Jesus' conversation with Martha (John 11:21f) and his discussion with Mary (Luke 10:38). Whatever else we may think of this latter story (today our first reaction may be to wonder why he didn't grab a tea towel and go and help Martha), Jesus is forcefully rejecting the conventional stereotyped role of women and saying very emphatically that they are called to the same intellectual and spiritual life as men. He praises Mary who sat at his feet and listened to his teaching for having "chosen the better part" and promises "it shall not be taken from her."

And notice, incidentally, the easy relaxed relationship among the three friends. The women feel completely free to complain to him.

Far from thinking that women are not worthy to learn about God, Jesus actually compares God to a woman! In Luke 15:8 God is a woman carefully cleaning her house, looking for a lost coin.

Finally, note that Jesus' female followers remain faithful to him at the end. The male disciples flee the crucifixion scene, but the women stay. On the third day after his death they are there to anoint his body.

THE RESURRECTION CONNECTION

The connection between women and the resurrection stories in the gospels is so dramatic that once having seen it you wonder how it can have been so long overlooked. As Swidler says in his article "Jesus Was a Feminist," "It is an overwhelming tribute to man's intellectual myopia not to have discerned it effectively in 2,000 years."[10]

There are three accounts of people being raised from the dead in the gospels, and they all intimately involve women. First, Jesus raised Jairus' daughter. In the second instance Jesus raised the only son of the widow of Nain. He did it because "when he saw her he had compassion on her and he said to her 'Do not weep.' " And he raised Lazarus from the dead at the request of Mary and Martha. They both pleaded with him and "When Jesus saw her (Mary) weeping and the Jews who came with her also weeping he was deeply moved in spirit and troubled... Jesus wept."

Jesus, then, raised one woman from the dead, and two others because of his feeling for the women involved. There are two further details here worth noting. With Jairus' daughter Jesus makes himself ritually unclean by touching the corpse. He does not feel it necessary to touch the men. Why?

In the story of Lazarus, Jesus talks to Martha about the resurrection and he declares himself to be "the resurrection and the life." Again we may wonder why he chose to disclose this central message about himself to this woman.

In the end it was to a woman (or women) that Jesus chose to reveal himself after his resurrection. All four gospels are clear on that point. And it was a woman (or women) whom he told to announce his resurrection to the men! The men typically did not believe it. They regarded it as "an idle tale" and went to see for themselves. Women in that society were not legally allowed to bear witness and for Jesus to have chosen them as his first witnesses was highly unusual and could have been nothing less than a conscious decision. Was it then his final affirmation of their equal status?

•

Women seem to have played a full and active part in the very early church and only during the last part of the first century, as the church began to accommodate itself to the patriarchal mores of the society, were they forced back into a subordinate position.[11] It may be that the church through the ensuing centuries has tended to see the women in the gospel as equations of Eve/sex/sin (or read here Mary Magdalene of whom there is absolutely no evidence of sexual misconduct. At most she was neurotic). Or equations of Mary/holiness/purity. Or has seen them only in relation to the men in the stories. Consequently we may have failed to see them as Jesus did, as whole persons. It was invariably as whole persons that Jesus responded to them.

•

"If we are not all liberated in Christ no one is liberated." (Rachel Conrad Wahlberg).

It was the summer of 1964 in the tiny prairie hamlet of Sedalia, Alberta. The dawn was just beginning to filter through the curtains of our 1 1/2 room summer student manse as we reluctantly packed up our arguments and went to bed. We had been reading Simone de Beauvoir's *The Second Sex.* We couldn't think why we'd brought it, but since it was one of the few books we had, we read it. And after a few pages stopped to ask each other if she could possibly be right. If it were true that women were totally equal and not properly dependent and subordinate, the implications were both frightening and exhilarating. (But what alternatives were there to the rosy role description of the cherished little woman working for a few years and then settling into happy domesticity with the wise, strong, protective male provider?) Later in the sixties, the experience was called consciousness raising. For us it was permanently unsettling.

Our experience was not, of course, in any way unusual. It happened thousands of times during those years. It was a grass roots revolution which is still going on. Couples are still, sometimes painfully, having to work out fair arrangements for sharing the child care and domestic duties and balancing work outside and inside the home, or more simply, deciding who's responsible for the rotten onion in the bottom of the fridge.

Accompanying changes in roles and ways of seeing ourselves was the realization that the structures of our society would also have to change. The present work situation, for example, assumes a large support system at home, particularly if there are children. But if both husband and wife take part-time jobs they lose out on most work benefits. The whole range of problems faced by women who work outside the home, particularly if they must work for a living (and most working women are still in that category) become more visible, - lack of adequate day care and maternity benefits, low wages and lack of wage equity, few advancement opportunities or exclusion from many jobs, restricted access to credit, and the wide-ranging problems of women's equal treatment before and protection under the law. The problems are far from solved. (Fact: in 1981 women in Canada earned fifty-eight cents to every dollar earned by a man.)[12]

In the church, Christian feminists began rigorous questioning of male interpretations of scripture, pulling out some fascinating but blurred stories of women's religious history, e.g. the prophetess Miriam, who may have been not Moses' and Aaron's sister but a co-leader, and the first century prophetess from Thyatira mentioned in Revelation.[13] They began pointing out the injustice of exclusive language, "As brothers of the Son of Man rise up O men of God." (It may be merely an accepted manner of speech but can you conceive of saying "womankind" and men placidly agreeing that they were included?) And it meant looking at church doctrines from a woman's viewpoint. Sin, for example, has been identified with pride, lust, aggressiveness, but, suggests Rachel Conrad Wahlberg in *Jesus According to a Woman,* this indicates what men feel guilty about. "Women, like blacks, have been cautioned to hold back, to be subject, suffer quietly in this world and do menial jobs. Thus, women's sin is to be self-denying, self-demeaning, reluctant to admit strength and God-given creativity and potential."[14]

A few Christian feminists are also pointing out that this current wave of freedom should involve not only changes in personal role consciousness and in the structures of society but, if it is healthy, will include a growing critical self awareness. It will mean the realization that "we are not simply 'the oppressed' or 'oppressors' but people who are sometimes one and sometimes the other in different contexts." It will mean recognizing that we all carry within ourselves a large capacity for oppression. You might say it means the realization of sin.

Reuther says "This is a blow to the ego of adolescent revolutionary personalities. But in the long run only this more complex self-knowledge gives us hope that liberation movements will not run merely to the reversal of hatreds and oppressions, but rather, to a recovery of greater humanity for us all."[15]

What the feminist movement has done for us, both men and women, is open around us large new spaces for living and a whole new range of options.

In the process of self-discovery, women may well realize that the jobs they've been doing all along are among the most important, that "If the real work of the world is that which extends into the future, that which is not ephemeral, and that which sustains life, we are talking about poetry and bread and babies" (Barbara G. Harrison in the October issue of *Harpers,* 1981). But they can be happy, too, that homemaking is not the only choice available to them.

And men, still enjoying their physical strength but no longer required to be bastions of forcefulness, may discover the beauty of gentleness, tenderness and vulnerability.

What both women and men can be certain of is that in their struggle to build more just social structures, the Jesus of the gospels is with them, and in their search for more equitable ways of relating to each other, he gives them his blessing.

# CHAPTER FIVE
# LIFE FOR THE GOOD PEOPLE

"For by grace you have been saved through faith; and this is not your own doing, it is the gift of God - Not because of works, lest anyone should boast...."

*Ephesians 2: 8-9*

"I danced for the scribe and the pharisee,
but they would not dance and they wouldn't follow me;
I danced for the fishermen, for James and John;
they came with me and the dance went on."

*Sydney Carter*

If in the gospels the poor have the centre stage, the scribes and Pharisees and later the priests and Sadducees form a sub-plot which gradually gathers momentum and finally blasts out the main theme. Jesus' encounters with some of the more respectable people of his day were stormy, antagonistic and tragic. He says to them, "the tax collectors and the harlots go into the Kingdom of God before you" (Matt 21:31), but some scholars argue that a more accurate translation of this text is "the tax collectors and the harlots go into the Kingdom of God *and not you.*"[1]

We might ask then if the Kingdom is only for the poor. If

you were not then, and, by extension are not now, in any significant way poor, are your hopes of heaven negligible? This type of exclusivism would seem to contradict everything Jesus was about. Jesus saw the narrow favouring of one group and the attendant attitudes of superiority as among the greatest evils of his society. He valued every human being equally, regardless of the person's wealth, power, prestige, or lack of it. And Jesus, as we have seen, urged all Jews to be a part of God's Kingdom on earth. The fact is that most of the respectable people rejected him, and in the end Jesus had to accept that. The implications of this are serious, particularly for those of us who might be numbered among the good and respected in our own society.

WHO WERE THEY?

Among the religious people of Jesus' day there were a number of clearly defined factions. The main ones were:
- the priests, whose position was hereditary and who conducted public worship in the temple in Jerusalem
- the Sadducees, the wealthy aristocracy who controlled the temple and the ruling council of the Jews
- the Pharisees, a strict religious sect
- the scribes, who were the trained theologians of both the Sadducees and Pharisees and acted as judges, making binding decisions on religious and penal law.

Jesus came into conflict with all these groups, but since he had most to do with and the most to say about "the Pharisees," it is mainly to this group we shall turn our attention here.

THE PHARISEES

A number of biblical scholars are now strongly contending that the Christian Church, beginning with the gospel writers has been sadly anti-semitic, particularly in regard to the Pharisees.[2] The gospels were written at a time when the conflict between Jewish and Jewish-Christian communities was stark and often ugly. After the destruction of Jerusalem

(A.D. 70), the Pharisees became the leaders of the Jewish communities; even before that period they would have been among those most opposed to major changes in the practice of their faith. The Pharisees, then, were the most hostile opponents of the early church. Jesus' conflicts may have been, in fact, with groups or individuals who were not Pharisees, and with certain individual Pharisees.[3] In the rabbinical writings of that period, some Pharisees are criticized as narrowly legalistic and hypocritical, but the Pharisees as a group are regarded as genuinely thoughtful and holy men.[4] It may have been because of their antagonism to the first Christians rather than to Jesus that they emerge in the gospels as the dominant, labelled enemy faction. It is a label which has stuck, to the extent that the Oxford Dictionary today defines "Pharisee" as "hypocrite."

As they do loom so large in our records, it's worth looking briefly at their background.

They were part of a people who had been chosen by God. God had rescued them from Egypt and nurtured them in law and mercy. But, as we are all too prone to do, they had fallen away from God repeatedly, until finally, they believed, they were punished by being exiled to Babylon. For the nation it was a shattering experience. When they returned to Palestine, serious Jews felt they had no option but to hold to the law and covenant with both hands. It was out of this conviction that Pharisaism arose.

In the second half of the second century B.C., Judaism was seriously in danger of being absorbed into Greek civilization. The Pharisees formed themselves into a band of "holy ones," "separate ones," who would preserve their Jewish traditions. They were largely successful, and over many generations proved themselves capable of great courage. When, for example, the Romans conquered Palestine, they as a group refused to sign the oath of allegiance to Caesar because they had only one lord, Yahweh. The Romans waived the oath for all Jews.[5] The Pharisees came from all social strata but were mostly merchants and craftsmen. Their numbers were always small, about 6,000 in Jesus' time, and their influence was disproportionately large.⁶ It's probable that the rabbis of the synagogues were trained in the Pharisaic interpretation of the law and this is what would have been taught boys like Jesus in the schools.

Jesus almost certainly regarded them as closer to the Kingdom than any other religious group in the society of his day. His own teachings, though more radical, were in form and content, Pharisaic. This would account, then, for his impatience with the spiritual blindness of certain Pharisees. As one modern Jewish scholar has commented, Jesus' remarks have all the raw harshness of in-family fighting, "a family quarrel."⁷ Nevertheless, the conflict was real and cannot honestly be slurred over. It makes his death more intelligible and maps out for us Jesus' basic teaching, his way of life. The essential is that we can't regard the conflict as being with a certain Jewish sect. It was a conflict with individuals, and even more, it is a conflict with us. We are "the Pharisees." Their sins are our sins. In the gospels they serve only to show us the cliff edges over which we so often slip.

## SIN/SINS

Jesus' principal and overriding criticism of these people was that they didn't take sin seriously. They put sins into neat manageable packages and then disposed of them. They saw sin as separate, individual sins. Sin was the breaking of one of the 613 commands or prohibitions of the Torah or one of their traditions. It was not seen as a condition which permeates all motives and actions, as a separation from God. Their principal object in life was to avoid breaking any of the rules, particularly the more serious ones (sins were finely graded). But if a sin were committed it could be counterbalanced by a good work, such as almsgiving.

It was the same attitude of mind that Martin Luther objected to so strongly in the church of the sixteenth century. A popular ditty of his day ran "When the coin in the coffer rings, the soul from purgatory springs." By careful calculation these Pharisees could be sure that on the day of judgment they (but certainly not "the sinners") would have more merits than demerits.

From Jesus' perspective they didn't take God seriously. They didn't have to. Their dealings with God were already satisfactorily concluded. And they often didn't take their neighbour seriously. As long as none of the major rules was broken there was no absolute need to. Their religion frequently resulted in an attitude of superiority, callousness, and lovelessness. But Jesus was also more specific in his criticism of them: "I tell you, on the day of judgment men will render account for every careless word they utter..." (Matt. 12:36)

THEY TALKED TOO MUCH

Their comments run like an angry counterpoint through the gospel narratives. When Jesus heals a dumb demoniac the crowd cries "Never was anything like this seen in Israel," but his critics mutter, "He casts out demons by the prince of demons" (Matt. 9:32). He heals a blind and dumb demoniac and "all the people were amazed" but they say "It is only by Beelzebub, the prince of demons, that this man casts out demons" (Matt. 12:24).

They ask:

"Why are they (the disciples) doing what is not lawful on the Sabbath" (Mark 2:24)?

"Why does he eat with tax collectors and sinners" (Mark 2:15)?

"Why do your disciples transgress the tradition of the elders" (Matt. 15:2)?

With time they become more aggressive. They set traps for him:

"Is it lawful to heal on the Sabbath" (Matt. 12:10)?

"Is it lawful for a man to divorce his wife" (Mark 10:2)?

"Is it lawful to pay taxes to Caesar" (Matt. 22:17)?

And finally they "took counsel against him, how to destroy him" (Matt. 12:14).

Jesus insisted that moral judgments be directed at deeds or attitudes, not at individuals: "Judge not, that you be not judged" (Matt. 7:1). "To call your brother 'fool' is to bring down fire on your head" (Matt. 5:22).

Although these people were sincerely concerned with the preservation and practice of their traditions, their words often reflect narrow cramped spirits. They were like the elder brother in the parable of the prodigal son. He resents the love his father lavishes on his undeserving younger brother. He's the only one who won't come in to the feast. You might say they were invited to a glorious, once-in-history party and they sat around making picky comments about the food.

THEY LOVED MONEY

"Do not lay up for yourselves treasures on earth" (Matt. 6:19).

Jesus was a realist. He knew that a person has to make a living and would have been the last to put down the people who work hard to support themselves or provide food, clothes and housing for a family. Jesus never idealized poverty and in fact his whole concern was that no one should be in want. He told people to pray for their daily needs ("Give us this day our daily bread" Matt. 6:11). But he saw clearly the crippling stress of worry about physical needs ("Therefore do not be anxious about tomorrow," Matt. 6:34). He knew how easily "the cares of the world and the delight in riches, and the desire for other things" (Mark 4:19) can choke out all thoughts of God. And he insisted that life must be more than a home in the suburbs with a finished basement, nutritious meals, pleasant holidays, and a comfortable bank balance. "A man's life does not consist in the abundance of his possessions" (Luke 12:15).

His teachings on money were considered among his "hardest" and in fairness to him, we ought not to soften and domesticate them. In Luke, Jesus makes it clear that the rich, as long as they are rich, have no place in the Kingdom. "Woe to you that are rich, for you have received your consolation. Woe to you that are full now for you shall hunger" (Luke 6:24-25).

Jesus says only a miracle is able to save the rich, and it is evident from the context, the story of the rich young ruler, that the miracle will not be getting the rich man into the Kingdom with his wealth but in getting him to give up his wealth. In the parable of the rich man and the beggar Lazarus, there is no reason why the rich man should have been excluded from the Kingdom except that he was rich (Luke 16:19f).

But how rich, then, is rich? Zacchaeus gives away half of what he owns and pays back four times what he has stolen. In the early Christian community where they were obviously striving to live out Jesus' teachings, "no one said that any of the things which he possessed was his own, but they had everything in common." "They sold their possessions and goods and distributed them to all, as any had need" (Acts 4:32, 2:45). They still met in each other's houses, so it doesn't mean they sold absolutely everything. Besides their houses they must still have had their own clothing, bedding, pots and pans. When it says "as many as were possessors of lands or houses sold them, and brought the proceeds of what was sold and laid it at the apostles' feet" (Acts 4:34-35), it probably means houses rented out and surplus land, their extra real estate and investments. So it meant giving up the surplus and treating nothing as your own, a carefree detachment toward possessions and an open generosity. Anyone in the community who was in need had a claim on your goods. Jesus had dared to envisage a world-wide community where there would be no rich or poor.

Here he clashed violently with some of the Pharisees. He accused them of rapacity and greed (Matt. 23:25). He says you cannot love God and money, and "The Pharisees, who loved money, heard all this and laughed at him. He said to them, 'You are the very ones who pass yourselves off as virtuous in people's sight, but God knows your hearts. For what is thought highly of by men is loathsome in the sight of God' " (Luke 16:14-15, Jerusalem Bible). Presumably one of those things thought highly of was wealth.

THEY BLEW THEIR OWN TRUMPETS

"Many that are first will be last, and the last first" (Mark 10:31).

Jesus was critical of people who hungered for social status and, seemingly, being included among the better people was another of those ideas enjoyed by "men" but hated by God. Among the better people Jesus had no reputation at all. Of certain Pharisees he says: they loved the best seats in the synagogues and being greeted in the market place (Luke 11:43). At dinner parties, they rushed to the places of honour (Luke 14:7).

To be thought well of in that society (apart from having hereditary wealth and power), one needed to be seen as a pious man. Accordingly these men, says Jesus with a gleam of humour in his eye, blow their trumpet in the street before they give alms, pray where they are most visible and when they fast, mark their faces so everyone will be suitably impressed. And, adds Jesus, they have their reward, their only reward, the praise of other people.

His comments are unequivocal. "Woe to you when all men speak well of you" (Luke 6:26). He himself refuses to be labelled good (Mark 10: 18). To his followers he says: don't let your right hand know what your left hand is doing; pray to your Father in secret. When people do see your good works they should give glory to God. If the glory comes back to you, the thing has gone wrong (Matt. 6:3,6, 5:16). Do not judge by appearances (John 7:24).

These Pharisees, in their push for respectability, he accuses of hypocrisy and shallowness. They have replaced inward goodness with superficial gestures. "Woe to you scribes and Pharisees, hypocrites! For you are like whitewashed tombs which outwardly appear beautiful, but within they are full of dead men's bones and all uncleanness. So you also outwardly appear righteous to men, but within you are full of hypocrisy and iniquity" (Matt. 23: 27-28).

For those who want to be highly regarded, he stands in front of them a child, a person of no status. The child is a live parable of powerlessness. "Whoever does not receive the Kingdom of God like a child shall not enter it" (Mark 10:15). "If anyone would be first he must be last of all and servant of all" (Mark 9:35). The only way to be great, says Jesus, is to be quietly serviceable.

THEY TRUSTED TOO MUCH IN THEIR OWN RIGHTEOUSNESS

"No one is good but God alone" (Mark 10:18).

While these Pharisees may have courted the approval of their betters, they knew well that they were acceptable to God, and a definite cut above the ordinary run of the population. Luke says that Jesus told them this parable because they "trusted in themselves that they were righteous and despised others" (Luke 18:9f).

A Pharisee, who may otherwise have led a blameless life, goes up to the temple to pray and casting sidelong glances at a neighbouring tax collector, thanks God that he is not like him. The tax collector, who makes no mention of reforming his ways, keeps his eyes on the ground and asks for God's mercy.

Jesus' conclusion must have shocked many of his listeners. "I tell you this man (the tax collector) went down to his house justified rather than the other, for everyone who exalts himself will be humbled but he who humbles himself will be exalted."

Paul, himself a Pharisee, probably stated the matter as succinctly as anyone: "We are justified (made right with God) by faith" (Romans 5:1). The one thing that can save us is our trust in God's mercy, for God does love us even though we don't deserve it. Paul called this undeserved love of God "grace." We can never work our way into God's favour. It is only God's enormous goodness that can reach out to us and make us whole. And it is out of gratitude to God that we reach out to our neighbour. Those who see themselves as needing little forgiveness, love little.

Those who are well (read: think they are well), says Jesus, need no physician, but those who (know they) are sick (Matt. 9:12). Jesus had found that there was nothing as impervious to change, nothing that blocked out the love of God so effectively, as religious zeal, piety and good works. Self-righteousness makes us smugly superior, and Jesus' antidote for that is humility: "everyone who humbles himself" (Luke 14:11). By humility he could not have meant an affected modesty about one's abilities, or even less a grovelling self-contempt, but most probably a recognition that even at my best, when I am most compassionate, forgiving and non-judgmental, I am still very far from whole and badly in need of God's help.

In looking at "the Pharisees," it's too easy for us to be Pharisaical and to thank God that we are not like them. It's too easy to forget that on a human level they were setting very high standards for themselves. And we forget that on a spiritual level, pride in being free from the law is no different from pride in obeying the law.

What Jesus made very clear was that anyone who has to feel superior to at least some people will feel very uncomfortable in the Kingdom of God.

THEY OPPRESSED THE POOR

"You shall love your neighbour as yourself" (Mark 12:31).

Jesus says that, having enslaved themselves to the law, they enslave others, convincing them that they must keep to the letter of the law or be damned. He says, "They bind heavy burdens, hard to bear, and lay them on men's shoulders; but they themselves will not move them with their finger" (Matt. 23:4). "But woe to you scribes and Pharisees, hypocrites! because you shut the Kingdom of Heaven against men; for you neither enter yourselves, nor allow those who would enter to go in" (Matt. 23:13). He says they tithe even the herbs in their garden but neglect justice (Matt. 23:23). They "devour widows' houses" (23:14), make excuses for not looking after their elderly parents, "and many such things you do" (Mark 7:10f). And on more than one occasion he tells them to find out what this means, "I (God) desire mercy and not sacrifice" (Matt. 9:13, 12:7). Coming from one who saw his life's work as setting free those who are oppressed, who summed up all the law and the prophets as loving God and one's neighbour, there could be no more serious charge. Paul again was to echo his words later in the century - even if I give my body to be burned and am not loving, I am nothing (I Cor. 13:3).

## THEY ASKED FOR SIGNS

"If you are the Christ, tell us plainly" (John 10:24).

Jesus was like many scribes or teachers of his day. He gathered around himself a group of pupils, debated points of law, was approached for decisions on points of law, preached at synagogue services and was addressed as Rabbi, but he didn't have the proper qualifications. He hadn't studied theology formally (John 7:15) and he wasn't ordained as scribes were.[8] He was also scandalously free with the law, criticizing it, even overruling it "You have heard that it was said... But I say to you...." (Matt. 5:21, 27, 31, 33, 38).

He sounded like a good man, but he was too flexible. He didn't fit the mould; he kept breaking the rules. He healed on the Sabbath and allowed his disciples to pick grain. He associated with the wrong sorts of people and had women friends. And he made highly questionable statements about prosperity, respectability, piety, and even family loyalty. He praised foreigners and said the whole nation (and not just the appropriate segments) was in danger of being destroyed. Many of the people thought he was a prophet. Some of the Pharisees weren't sure, not surprisingly, since his family also thought his activities extremely dubious and his friends said "he is beside himself" (Mark 3:21).

These Pharisees kept asking for a sign, not a simple miracle, but a spectacular wonder which would prove beyond any doubt that Jesus was a man of God. Jesus consistently refused to perform (Mark 8:11-13, Luke 11:16f, John 2:18f, 4:48, 6:30f).

They suspected he was a blasphemer and that he was usurping the authority of God. They said he "called God his Father making himself equal with God" (John 5:18). The people said that by his authority he cast out demons and that "he taught them as one who had authority and not as the scribes'' (Mark 1:22). Who did he think he was?

Jesus never went about publicly claiming to be God. What he did claim was that he spoke the truth and he spoke it out of his close relationship with God. Further than that, his words and actions had to speak for themselves, to be self-authenticating. They had to be seen as good and true in themselves - and just that. There was no other proof that they were from God.

On one level, you might say that Jesus' critics were lacking imagination. They simply couldn't see how God's Spirit could be working through a man like Jesus. Jesus, however, in this context, accused them of the final sin, the sin against the Holy Spirit. They were trying to define and confine God, rejecting God's work when they found it in unexpected places and calling it unclean. To this Jesus says, " 'whoever blasphemes against the Holy Spirit never has forgiveness, but is guilty of an eternal sin' - for they had said, 'He has an unclean spirit' " (Mark 3:29-30).

It was on a charge of blasphemy that they finally conspired with others to have him arrested and killed.

DID JESUS LOVE THE PHARISEES?

One doesn't have to be very delicate to squirm inwardly over Jesus' diatribe against the Pharisees. It's hard to imagine how he could have been more harsh or uncompromising. We might even wonder whether he who said you must love your enemies loved his. It's obvious, however, from looking at the gospels as a whole that he kept reaching out to them. He eats with them (Luke 7:36, 11:37, 14:1). He continually argues with them, and his best, most loving detailed stories are told for their benefit (e.g. the lost sheep, the lost coin, the prodigal son, Luke 15:4f; Dives and Lazarus, Luke 16:19; the Pharisee and the tax collector, Luke 18:9f). In the parable of the banquet (Luke 14:16f), they are the first invited. In the parable of the prodigal son, the father says to the elder brother (the Pharisees) "All that is mine is yours" (Luke 15:31).

His sympathy and concern for them is often evident. When they want a sign "he sighed deeply in his spirit" (Mark 8:11). He "grieved at their hardness of heart" (Mark 3:5). And at the end of Matthew's long list of "Woe unto you" in chapter 23, he has Jesus crying over Jerusalem, "I would have gathered your children together as a hen gathers her brood under her wings, and you would not" (Matt 23:37)!

Even at their most scathing, his words are not those of someone who has written off a group of people.

Jesus' loving was not cheap and easy. He found that loving one group often necessitated conflict with another group and that love didn't exclude anger and confrontation. Because he cared about these Pharisees didn't mean he approved of what they did. And should we ever be tempted to think too facilely of reconciliation, it's worth remembering that Jesus never was reconciled to them. He was unable to break through their hard religious crust and bring them the life that he was promising to their poorer and less religious brothers and sisters.

THE DISCIPLES

"Your names are written in heaven" (Luke 10:20).

The disciples form another group which has some claim to being the "good people." They were not among the most respected elements of society (some, like Matthew, the tax collector, were included among the "sinners") but they were serious about their faith and provide an interesting comparison with the Pharisees.

Many biblical scholars argue that the disciples were not always the set group of twelve we have imagined but in the gospels the word "disciples" often refers to Jesus' followers generally, as for example when Luke speaks of "the whole multitude of the disciples" (Luke 19:37).[9] Certainly Jesus was continually calling people to become his disciples and setting the same high demands for them all. There were no first and second-class followers. He required from each of them an absolute allegiance. "He who loves father or mother more than me is not worthy of me and he who does not take up his cross and follow me is not worthy of me" (Matt. 10:37).

We have also tended to think of the disciples as a happy and devoted enclave, but it is impossible to read very far into the gospels before realizing that they and Jesus had some rather major areas of conflict.

They had given up everything to follow him. They had the benefit of Jesus' personal teaching. ("Privately to his disciples he explained everything" Mark 4:34.) They were with him for long periods of time, hearing him preach, watching him heal. Some of them were alone with him in moments of crisis and high drama (e.g. on the Mount of Transfiguration, Matt. 17, the raising of Jairus' daughter, Mark 5:22f, the garden of Gethsemane, Mark 14:32f). But they often seem to have misunderstood what he was about. When Jesus speaks of the "leaven of the Pharisees" they think he's talking about bread, and Jesus rounds on them, "Do you not yet perceive or understand? Are your hearts hardened? Having eyes do you not see, and having ears do you not hear? And do you not remember" (Mark 8:15f)? When they ask him about the parable of the sower, Jesus comments, "Do you not understand this parable? Then how will you understand all the parables" (Mark 4:13)?

They object to Jesus' teaching on divorce, that it is too hard (Matt. 19:10). They are "greatly astonished" at Jesus' teaching on money (Matt. 19:25). They are "indignant" when the woman pours the ointment over Jesus' feet (Matt. 26:8) and Jesus is "indignant" when they send away the mothers and children (Mark 10:14). When Jesus tells them he is going up to Jerusalem to die, Peter objects strongly and Jesus rejoins, "Get behind me Satan! You are a hindrance to me; for you are not on the side of God, but of men" (Matt. 16:23).

Their faith falters. They can't heal the epileptic and Jesus cries, "O faithless generation, how long am I to be with you? How long am I to bear with you" (Mark 9:19)? They are frightened in the storm and Jesus asks, "Why are you afraid, O men of little faith" (Matt. 8:26)?

They ask the wrong sorts of questions. "Who is the greatest in the Kingdom of Heaven" (Matt. 18:1)? "How

often shall my brother sin against me and I forgive him"
(Matt. 18:21)?

Their misunderstandings and Jesus' replies form another
of those threads that weave through the gospel stories until
even after the resurrection Jesus is saying to them, "O foolish
men and slow of heart" (Luke 24:25).

They are not conspicuous for their courage. In the garden
of Gethsemane, they all run away. At the trial, Peter curses
and swears that he doesn't know Jesus. They don't attend the
crucifixion.

But to them Jesus also says, "To you it has been given to
know the secrets of the Kingdom of Heaven" (Matt. 13:11).
What they had to commend them was their faith. In the
beginning Andrew shouts to Peter, "We have found the
Messiah" (John 1:41), and later Peter declares to Jesus,
"You are the Christ, the son of the living God" (Matt.
16:16).

Jesus called them and they immediately left their nets and
followed. He sent them out to teach and heal and they went.
He told them to go into all the world and preach the gospel
and they did. Their faith was the means by which Jesus could
change their lives and spread his life-giving Spirit across the
earth and down through time. In spite of what they may have
got wrong, they got that one thing right, and even if their
faith did at times falter, it was the one thing needed.

# CHAPTER SIX
# WAS JESUS A REVOLUTIONARY?

"And he entered the temple and began to drive out those who sold and those who bought in the temple, and he overturned the tables of the money-changers and the seats of those who sold pigeons; and he would not allow anyone to carry anything through the temple. And he taught, and said to them, 'Is it not written, My house shall be called a house of prayer for all the nations? But you have made it a den of robbers.' And the chief priests and the scribes heard it and sought a way to destroy him; for they feared him, because all the multitude was astonished at his teaching."

*Mark 11:15-18*

"The disciple of Jesus is, more than anyone else, a political animal condemned to death; he cannot be greater than his Master."

*Sebastian Kappen (Indian theologian)*

The manager of the Durban Christian Guest Home was sobbing out a story of missionary friends, killed by Mugabe "terrorists" in Rhodesia the night before. Our children sat round-eyed and unnaturally still as she stumbled through a long tearful prayer for the repose of the dead and the conversion of their murderers. And at the end of it our seven-year-old whispered urgently across the breakfast table, "Who are the terrorists?"

"The guerrillas."

We watched helplessly as understanding turned to bewilderment.

"You mean the freedom fighters?"

We nodded.

The freedom fighters were his heroes. His room was papered with revolutionary posters, and being an inveterate eavesdropper, he had listened to a number of hot conversations by university students: South Africans, Rhodesians and others. Should they sacrifice their schooling to join the guerrillas? The Christians among them agonized over "Blessed are the peacemakers" and "I have come to set at liberty those who are oppressed." And while the most frivolous students, when school work became onerous, threatened to "go to the bush," it was usually the most idealistic who went.

Watching the uprising of the Third World, many of us share his confusion. Where is the right and wrong, or even, in some instances, the "right" and the "left"? And while certainly some organizations and some governments are more humane than others, and the Zimbabwe Patriotic Front could not be numbered among the worst, few would deny that atrocities occur on all sides. For us, understanding may mean a difficult and concerted effort to sort out the issues. But for many of our Christian sisters and brothers caught up in situations of violence, the questions are necessarily urgent and practical. How would Jesus react in a highly oppressive or revolutionary situation? Can a Christian join the guerrillas? Was Jesus himself a revolutionary? It is against questions such as these that we shall look at Jesus' involvement in the politics of the day.

JESUS AS REVOLUTIONARY

Jesus' resemblance to present-day revolutionaries cannot be denied. He was passionately concerned with the welfare of the common people, to the extent of fatally antagonizing the authorities, and he was interested in their gritty everyday needs, not merely in their souls. His words in John, "My kingship is not of this world" (John 18:36), have to be interpreted in light of how John elsewhere uses the term "this world.'' It means how things are normally done, the accepted standards and practices. Jesus is saying his kingdom cannot simply be equated with ordinary earthly kingdoms. But it certainly had large political implications.

It has to be remembered, too, that the Jews would not have thought in terms of "religion" and "politics." A secular problem would have been unthinkable. Everything that was done in that society was supposedly done according to God's will, God's law. Religious authorities were political leaders. To attack the religious authorities and religious practices was to be immediately involved in political dissent.[1]

But Jesus made it abundantly clear that what he wanted was a thorough wash of the social fabric, root-deep changes in the way people related to each other, and, inevitably, a radical revision of religious practices, economics and politics. He wanted to upturn the whole of society, and that's not a religious revival. That's a revolution.*

He knew what it was to be on the run and in hiding. The authorities send spies to infiltrate and report on his gatherings (Luke 20: 19-20). After a point he can no longer travel openly (John 11:54). He has to leave Jerusalem and Judea (John 7:1) and is not safe in Galilee (Mark 9:30). He becomes a fugitive in the regions beyond Galilee. When he finally returns to Judea, he has to make complicated undercover arrangements to celebrate the passover meal (Mark 14:13). He spends the night outside the city in Bethany (Mark 11:11, 14:3), in Ephraim (John 11:54) and Gethsemane (Mark 14:32), and during the day he seeks safety in the crowds where he knows the authorities won't attempt to capture him for fear of riots (Mark 14:2, Luke 20:19).

Sam was a South African refugee. He had been interned on Robben Island and eventually escaped from prison in Pretoria. He was teaching in a high school in Lesotho but was informed one night that individual local police were prepared to turn him over to the

*A distinction should be made between a coup, where there is only a shifting of power, and a revolution, where what is wanted is a fundamental change in the structure of society.

South Africans. He walked twenty-five miles across country to our house. For three days he remained inconspicuous in our back bedroom. He also gave us detailed, highly instructive lessons on how to remain sane in solitary confinement. The essential is a self-enforced daily regime of activity. He was an English teacher, and so prepared and taught his classes with great dedication each day. This type of teaching, he said, had one outstanding advantage over ordinary classroom teaching. There were never any essays to mark. On the weekend he devised special forms of recreation - a five mile on-the-spot run.

Then on the fourth morning, camouflaged in a floppy hat of ours, he said he was going to see the editor of the church newspaper for advice. He never arrived there. Apparently he took a bus in the opposite direction to the border, then followed the "underground railroad" through South Africa to Botswana. A week later we received a telegram: "HEALTH MUCH IMPROVED IN GABARONE. SAM."

Jesus is finally arrested on a phony charge, and witnesses falsely testify against him (Mark 14:56). He is tortured (Matt. 27:26-32) and condemned as a traitor. He suffers a death normally reserved for revolutionaries and rebels of the Roman state: a slow, agonized and public death designed as a deterrent to the masses.

There is something smouldering fiercely within him. "I came to cast fire upon the earth and would that it were already kindled" (Luke 12:49). He frequently shows signs of ruthlessness evident in those who are determined on change. "No one who puts his hand to the plough and looks back is fit for the Kingdom of God" (Luke 9:62). In the immediacy of his cause, he rejects a concern for the dead that is as old as human life. "Leave the dead to bury their own dead" (Luke 9:60).

It's important not to undervalue the fundamentally rebellious, even militant side of Jesus. Admittedly he was capable of great tenderness, as when he was with the children, but his attacks upon the Pharisees should in themselves be enough to kill forever the popular image of "gentle Jesus meek and mild."

Yet he never killed anyone. He never led an organized revolt or resistance. What kind of revolutionary was he?

## JESUS AS CRIMINAL

His relation to the political authorities of his day is probably most evident in his arrest, trial and execution. The passion narratives cover roughly one third of the gospels and are obviously seen by the writers to be the pivotal point of the Jesus story.

The accounts of the passion in all four gospels are set in the same framework - the entry into Jerusalem, last supper, Gethsemane, arrest, hearing before the Sanhedrin, Peter's denial, the Barabbas story, condemnation by Pilate, crucifixion and burial - but the details are very different and difficult to assess. It is possible, however, to make a distinction about the possible charges, the actual charge, and the real motive for his death.

Some possible reasons for his execution are mentioned during the trial, and according to the New Testament scholar J. Jeremias, the Jews could have condemned him for a number of misdemeanours of which Jesus had plainly been accused during his ministry: practising magic, casting out demons with the help of Beelzebub (Matt. 12:24), blaspheming against God (Mark 2:7), being a false prophet (Mark 14:65), and deliberately breaking the Sabbath (Mark 2:24f, 3:5, 6).[2]

He was finally condemned for claiming to be a Messiah-king and so a threat to the Roman authority (Mark 15:26). The real motive, according to Mark and Matthew, was the envy or jealousy of the local authorities (Mark 15:10, Matt. 27:18).

The Sanhedrin, the Jewish court, consisting of the high priest and seventy chief priests, elders and scribes, heard the case, but it was the Roman court presided over by the Roman procurator Pilate which tried, sentenced and executed him. Why? What possible interest did the Romans have in this relatively harmless visionary?

## ACCORDING TO PILATE

Pilate was a particularly ruthless Roman procurator. He deliberately provoked the Jews, and when they rebelled, didn't hesitate to kill them, often without trial. Josephus, the first century historian, gives several examples, one being Pilate's appropriation of temple funds for an aqueduct. When the Jews protested, they were surrounded and battered with clubs. Many were killed or injured. Pilate also had a phobia about large gatherings.[3]

According to Philo, a Jewish philosopher of Jesus' day, Pilate was "by nature inflexible, self-willed and hard." He says Pilate was guilty of "bribery, tyranny, pillage, violence, calumny, constant execution without passing a verdict and endless insufferable cruelty." This agrees with Luke who speaks of "the Galileans whose blood Pilate mingled with that of their sacrifices" (in the temple?) (Luke 13:1).[4] We know other procurators summarily killed any potential prophets, and any popular movement was highly suspect. Pilate probably knew that Jesus was a popular leader and that many of his followers regarded him as a prophet if not the Messiah.

Jesus himself almost certainly disliked the Romans as much as any Palestinian did. He disapproved of the swaggering harshness of Roman rule, the way they lorded it over their subjects (Mark 10:42). He saw them as a threat and predicted that one day the eagles (the symbol of Rome) would peck at the Jewish carcass (Matt. 24:28). And there can be no question that he knew what a revolutionary was. His own province of Galilee was a traditional hotbed of revolutionary activity against the Romans. When Jesus was a child, the rebel leader Judas of Galilee had been crucified, together with two thousand of his followers.[5]

Many scholars believe that the Zealots, an organized group of Jewish nationalist guerrillas, were active in Jesus' day,[6] but there is no evidence that Jesus supported them. When asked about Roman taxation, Jesus said, "Render therefore to Caesar the things that are Caesar's, and to God the things that are God's" (Matt. 22:21). Since in the Jewish tradition what belonged to God was undivided loyalty, the statement is more subversive than it at first appears, and the implications would not have escaped Jesus' Jewish listeners. Jesus, however, was not openly opposing Roman rule. It's possible he rejected the idea of revolt as suicidal, but it's certain that he had a broader agenda than the overthrow of the Romans.

It's also certain that he was tempted by political leadership. John says that at one point about five thousand men came out to him asking him to become their leader, wanting to make him king (John 6:14-15). Jesus is sympathetic. He sees them as "a sheep without a shepherd." But he diffuses the situation, forces his disciples to get in a boat, and then goes off to the hills to pray (Mark 6:45-46, Matt. 14:22-23).

At Caesarea Philippi, Peter is annoyed at Jesus talking about himself as a suffering servant. The political power is there, available to him. Why doesn't he seize it? Jesus is angry with Peter for playing the tempter. "Get behind me Satan" (Matt. 16:23). The words are almost the same as those in the temptation story in Matthew 4:10, where Satan offers Jesus all the kingdoms of the world. It was a struggle. He must have considered all that he could have achieved with political power, but what he envisaged was a kingdom very different from the kingdoms of this world. To replace one group of people who misunderstood his intentions with another group who were equally oblivious would have made no difference. Without compassion, any politics would be oppressive.

Present day revolutionaries would talk of the problem in terms of "conscientization." Before changes can be effective, the majority of the people have to be made aware of the issues and convinced of the validity of change (conscientized). The idea of conscientization is very like the biblical concept of repentance. The word repentance means literally a turning around, a radical shift of ideas and feelings, and implies changes in action. Without adequate conscientization, a revolution flounders or resorts to internal violence. Without repentance, the Kingdom wouldn't come. Presumably, if the people had been willing to accept Jesus' vision of the Kingdom and had been prepared to change accordingly, he would have taken over the leadership as a Messiah/Servant/King. But it didn't happen.


ACCORDING TO THE JEWISH LEADERS

Whatever the Romans' role in the story may have been (in

John, Pilate goes through what must be one of the most useless little charades in history, washing his hands of the whole affair), the gospel writers are all in agreement that local people were mainly responsible for Jesus' death. Matthew, to reinforce his point, has them crying "His blood be on us and on our children" (Matt. 27:25). It was to prove an extremely unfortunate statement, an excuse for the horrors of anti-semitism over many centuries. Matthew's words have to be set against the fact that the authorities couldn't arrest Jesus for fear of the crowds and against Luke's more careful statement that at the crucifixion "the people stood by, watching, but the rulers scoffed" (Luke 23:35) and "All the multitudes who assembled to see the sight, when they saw what had taken place, returned home beating their breasts" (Luke 23:48).

The "Jews" were no more responsible for the death of Jesus than the "Greeks" were for the death of Socrates. The Jewish *authorities* were the ones who were implicated in Jesus' death. Jesus saw them more than the Romans as the real oppressors of the people and consequently confronted them.

We have detailed Jesus' conflict with the Pharisees in the previous chapter, and it would seem that very early on they determined to have him destroyed. By contemporary law a capital crime could only be brought to judgment if the perpetrator was warned and it was known to be deliberate.[7] Mark 2:24 reports a warning to Jesus regarding his breaking of the Sabbath, and that Jesus said he was breaking it out of conviction. With the next infringement he would be in mortal danger especially if he were watched, which he was (Mark 3:2). His death was decided by these men after the second breach of the Sabbath (Mark 3:6). Herod, who was the king of Galilee and had the power of execution there may have been informed of the charge, for Jesus was in real danger and was forced to flee the territory.

It was his cleansing of the temple, however, that finally set the authorities firmly against him. Traders were doing a roaring business in the temple court with the connivance of the Sadducees and priests who were probably taking their cut of the profit. Pilgrims had to change their currency into temple currency which alone could buy sacrificial animals and birds. The exorbitant rates of exchange and the high prices incensed Jesus. They were exploiting the devotion of the people - many of them poor like the woman with two coins. Jesus' reaction was coldly deliberate. He leaves, makes a whip and comes back the next day with supporters. He overturns the tables of the money-changers and the seats of those selling pigeons, and for a time will not allow anyone to use the temple court as a thoroughfare (Mark 11:15-19).

Etienne Trocmé, in a piece of scholarship that is both original and meticulous,[8] argues that the temple incident was not in the last week (as in Mark, Matthew and Luke) or at the beginning of Jesus' work (as in John) but probably a few weeks or months before the crucifixion and marked the watershed of his ministry. After this event, he was an acknowledged public figure and always on the run. Whenever, Jesus' action was a direct threat to the Jewish leadership and made it obvious that he had to be eliminated.

John has a graphic description of the Jewish court's (the Sanhedrin's) deliberations (John 11:45f). The Sanhedrin was composed mainly of Sadducees, who were not usually pious men like the Pharisees, but men of affairs, and collaborators with Rome. Their motive for wanting Jesus dead was stark expediency. It's possible that Pilate had already ordered them to hand Jesus over and this was a convenient case of extradition.[9] It's also possible that this was a preventive measure should Pilate question their ability to maintain control: "If we let him go on thus everyone will believe in him, and the Romans will come and destroy both our holy place and our nation" (John 11:48). It's also possible they simply feared for their positions if Jesus became too influential. Since only the Roman procurator could sentence a person to death in Judea,[10] they may have had to convince Pilate that Jesus should be executed. How Pilate must have secretly relished the chief priests begging him to kill this rebel against Rome and declaring "We have no king but Caesar" (John 19:15)!

The Greek word used for what they did was "hand over" or "betray." They were betraying a Jewish national to the

Roman occupation; eventually Roman and Jewish authorities arrived at a mutually satisfactory charge. Jesus (they said) claimed to be a Messiah-king, an accusation which meant blasphemy to the Jews and political revolt to the Romans.

Judas is also said to have betrayed Jesus, and it's interesting to speculate here on what precisely the betrayal was. What did he do for thirty pieces of silver? Possibly the money was given for information of Jesus' whereabouts and for identifying him. But thirty pieces of silver is a rather large sum of money. Could identification have been so difficult, and could their spies not easily have followed the group out of the city? Could the payment have also been for the information that Jesus secretly claimed to be the Messiah, and was unlikely to deny it publicly?

On a human level, one might say that Jesus was being caught up in what the Brazilian archbishop Helder Camara has called a "spiral of violence."[11] The situation is as common as dandelions in political affairs past and present. Institutional violence - unjust laws, unequal economic arrangements - leads to protest (violent or otherwise) which leads to even greater institutional violence - killings, torture, disappearances - which then leads to more revolutionary protest, and so on. Jesus protested and was killed. By befriending and defending the poor and powerless, he affronted the respectable ruling classes. By daring to criticize the Pharisees and offend the Sadducees, he took on the power establishment of the nation. By arousing the hatred of the local collaborators with the Romans, he implicitly took on the Roman authorities. By stirring up the crowd he directly threatened the renowned Roman peace. Did they have any choice?

According to the gospel writers, however, Jesus was not simply the tragic victim of a power play in a vicious system. He deliberately went up to Jerusalem to his death (Matt. 16:21). What did he think he was doing? What did he hope to accomplish?

## ACCORDING TO JESUS

Jesus did not think of himself as a revolutionary. He was in the line of the prophets. He says, "I must go on my way today and tomorrow and the day following, for it cannot be that a prophet should perish away from Jerusalem" (Luke 13:33). (See also Mark 6:4, Matt. 23:37-39, Luke 4:24.) And while prophets and revolutionaries may have many characteristics in common, they are quite separate breeds. One doesn't decide to become a prophet. One is called, and it is a job usually programmed for failure.

God sent the prophets of the Old Testament to protest against the people falling away and the consequent social, economic and political injustice of the nation. The prophets were demanding all that a revolutionary would in the way of social change. But they were also calling for a tenderness and compassion that would touch those whose problems cannot be eliminated by good economics and politics: the wife whose husband has left her, the terminally ill, the handicapped and elderly. The prophets were ignored, ridiculed, tortured, killed. The prophet immediately preceding Jesus, John the Baptist, was beheaded. Jesus, whose ministry began where John left off, (Mark 1:14) could not have expected any better treatment. There is overwhelming evidence in the gospels that Jesus predicted his own suffering and death and tried to prepare his disciples for a similar fate (Mark 8:31, 9:31, 10:33, 12:8 etc.).

Prophets are not expected to be successful. They are expected to be faithful, to persistently call people to repentance, and to accept the personal consequences. One might say then that Jesus died because that was what frequently happened to prophets. Whether Jesus thought of himself as more than a prophet and his death as having more importance has been strongly debated among biblical scholars.

He never publicly claimed the title of "Messiah," and even at his trial, when asked "Are you the Son of God?" gives a non-committal answer: "You say that I am" (Luke 22:70). But that is almost certainly because the Jews were expecting a particular kind of political Messiah and he refused to play that role. He speaks of himself as "Son of Man," a term to which his enemies never objected, and the Jewish scholar G. Vermes has shown was not a title but a modest way of referring to oneself, used instead of "I" in Galilean Aramaic.[12]

The Son of Man in Daniel 7, however, is very like the Messiah in other Old Testament writings, and some of the passages where Jesus employs it ("You will see the Son of Man seated at the right hand of Power, and coming on the clouds of heaven" - Matt. 26:64) definitely refer to Daniel. While Jesus undoubtedly used the term as Vermes has indicated, and emphasized it to show his solidarity with "man," all people, it probably also had Messianic overtones.

If Jesus thought of himself as the Messiah, then he also regarded his death as having a unique significance.

Death in Judaism had atoning power if bound up with repentance. If a criminal said "My death be an atonement for all my sins," he was forgiven. An unnatural death of a righteous man was more powerful and could even be an atonement for the sins of others. "Let my blood serve to cleanse them (the people of God). Take my life in place of theirs," prayed the old martyr Eleazar.[13] The suffering of a good man could make up for the sinfulness of many others. This was the tradition in which Jesus was steeped, and which is reflected in the words of the last supper: "this is my body.... this is my blood of the covenant, which is poured out for many for the forgiveness of sins" (Matt. 26:26-28). Jesus saw his death, too, as a "ransom for many" (Mark 10:45). These words link his death with the suffering servant passage in Isaiah 53. There the death of God's servant will be innocent (v.9), voluntary (v. 10), patiently borne (v.7), willed by God (vv. 6, 10), and therefore atoning for others (v. 4f). This life, because it was with God and from God, would in death, have an unlimited power to atone, to take on the consequences of our sinfulness.

In his earthly life, it was the last thing that Jesus could do for his people and for the Kingdom.


WAS JESUS A PACIFIST?

We are left, then, with the thorny problem of Jesus' attitude toward violence.

By violence, we mean inflicting pain or injury of any kind on human beings. The word usually summons up images of guns and guerrillas. But violence is more commonly structural and institutional. When governments and societies live by laws and economic arrangements which benefit some at the expense of others, this is violence. When economic and political systems discriminate against and humiliate whole races, classes, or even nations, this is violence. The violence of a system can be legal and respectable and yet impoverish human beings and frustrate their potential. Jesus was, with all the passion of his personality, opposed to this kind of institutionalized violence. But was he a pacifist in the sense of rejecting all physical conflict? Would he always oppose every kind of violent self-defense, or violent attack upon institutional violence? Some of his sayings are at least superficially contradictory, and it's crucial not to take them out of their context.

"Turn the other cheek" occurs in a passage about not seeking revenge, and must be a practical example of what loving the neighbour can sometimes mean (Matt. 5:39, Luke 6:29).

"I have not come to bring peace, but a sword" (Matt. 10:34) is part of a warning about persecution, and the disruption, particularly to family life, which will result from being his followers.

"All who take the sword will perish by the sword" (Matt. 26:52) is obviously not always a true prescription. In the circumstances in which it was said, the garden of Gethsemane, where they were surrounded by a Roman guard, resistance would have been suicidal.

Jesus tells his disciples to buy swords, even at great personal sacrifice: "Let him who has no sword sell his mantle and buy one" (Luke 22:36), but only when they were in danger and swords were presumably needed for self-defense.

What can be said of Jesus with some accuracy is that, although he was not a pacifist in principle, he was a remarkably peaceful man. He knew from his dealings with the religious authorities that the loving defense of one group sometimes necessitated confrontation and conflict with another group. His disciples are instructed to have swords, the money-changers are driven out of the temple, and his words to his enemies are anything but pacific. But it is also true that he hated violence and was predominantly a non-violent person. He went to his death with quiet acceptance. The peacemakers are the ones who are blessed. His followers are told "to love your enemies and pray for those who persecute you" (Matt. 5:44). And certainly, as Jesus saw, the Kingdom would not be ultimately brought in through violence but by faith and compassion.

Along the way, however, love of the neighbour may sometimes entail his or her violent defense. Jesus' basic ethic was not non-violence, but love. To sit passively and watch one person exploit another is to love neither the exploiter nor the exploited. Fighting the enemies may be a way of loving them and indeed may be the only way of putting relationships in order and destroying a false appearance of peace.[14] Violence, of course, must always remain abhorrent to Christians, and the last option, but to do nothing or to refuse to use physical violence may amount to co-operation with more subtle and more insidious forms of institutional violence.

We are back, then, with the problem with which we started. Where would Jesus stand in regard to the revolutionary movements of the present day? The truth can only be that wherever the oppressed are being liberated, he is there, and the one place we will never find him is sitting quietly on the sidelines.

# FROM DEATH TO LIFE

## I

### REFLECTIONS ON THE CROSS

"So they took Jesus, and he went out bearing his own
cross, to the place called the place of a skull, which is
called in Hebrew Golgotha. There they crucified him,
and with him two others, one on either side, and Jesus
between them."

*John 19: 17-18*

"The just will be whipped, stripped of their skin, tied
and blinded with fire. When they have suffered all these
pains, they will be nailed to a cross."

*Plato, The Republic, (2, 5, 361 E)*

One spring he must have smelt the fresh warmth of the air,
and realized that he would not smell it again. His last
Passover. The red flowers on the hills outside Jerusalem.
Consider the flowers of the fields and don't be anxious about
tomorrow. He who loses his life will save it. Life is more than
keeping yourself alive.

•

"Father forgive them," he says, and it is done. His blood is
shed for many for the forgiveness of sins. We are forgiven.

The relationship between God and humanity is radically changed. The whole of creation is redeemed. It can never be anything else.

•

"My God, my God, why have you forsaken me?" The endless mystery of why we suffer and die. But he has suffered and died with us and so we do not suffer and die alone. We are not abandoned.

•

"It is finished." And though it may be whispered in agony, it is a shout of victory. He has done what he set out to do. He knows when to stop.

•

But still we mourn him. He was a good man, and he shouldn't have died. He had integrity, courage, intelligence, that wildly generous love and, not a soft sentimental piety, but a spirituality. It was what formed him. Without it, we are tied to external activity and become inflexible slaves or indeterminate chameleons. Without it, action becomes shallow, a shower of sparks and discouraging. For even the poor and sinners are sinful, and those seeking justice are not perfectly just. In his room, on the hillsides, in the garden, on the cross, he spent time with his Father. He didn't talk much. Your Father knows what you need before you ask. So he must have been mostly listening. That was enough.

•

For two thousand years we've watched him on the cross. It reminds us that he died because of the way he lived. And it's difficult to make the cross a symbol of prestige, prosperity, or success. So the cross is all right as long as he isn't pinned there as a beautifully divine butterfly, unable to cry, "Woe to you who are full now," to drive the money-changers out of the temple, and cry and laugh with his friends.

•

They said he rose from the dead, of course, but that can't be proved. It's a miracle. We can only weigh in the evidence of the witnesses, five hundred at one time, James, the apostles, the women at the tomb. There are Peter and the other apostles, who fled from the Sanhedrin at Jesus' trial and later went back to declare to that august body: "We must obey God rather than men.... The God of our fathers raised Jesus, whom you killed by hanging him on a tree. God exalted him at his right hand as Leader and Saviour, to give repentance to Israel and forgiveness of sins. And we are witnesses to these things and so is the Holy Spirit whom God has given to those who obey him." There is finally the existence of the Christian Church.

# II

"Because I live, you will live also" (John 14:19).

We in the "West" have tended to think of the cross and resurrection in terms of the victory of good over evil, and of eternal life. The following are quotes and paraphrases of African, Asian, black American and Latin American writers on what they have called:

## THE POLITICS OF THE RESURRECTION

*"The resurrection rehabilitates Jesus before the world"* (Boff, Brazil).[1] He is not a criminal, but Emmanuel, God with us. His words, then, were not the words of a mad man, but the thoughts of God. His scale of values was not that of an impractical dreamer, but God's scale of values. His enthusiasms and loves are those of God. This is God and God is like this.

*"How different is this God of the pompous church and the militant missions from the God of the cross"* (Choan-Seng Song, China)![2] The God we encounter in Jesus is a God who suffers with the powerless and helpless. Indeed, "God is at the height of his power when he reaches the depth of

helplessness."[3] To be children of this God, then, is to be prepared to share God's suffering in the world, and to stand by those who suffer. "This is a dangerous theology. It is dangerous to the church, which is burdened with the glory and privilege of the past and feels constrained to retain its power and influence that have eroded in recent years.... It is (only) a suffering church that can give witness to the crucified God. The church that lives in affluence, the church that is contented with wealth and resources will find it difficult to be a crucified church of the crucified God."[4]

*"The resurrection is a political event"* (Cone, Black America).[5] The resurrection was an unparalleled political victory, and Jesus was the victor. Because the imperialists and local elite, the powerful of this world, lost that round, there is every hope that they will lose many more rounds and finally the last round. Not only their political, but their social and economic arrangements have been absolutely discredited. The poor "can know that their poverty is a contrived phenomenon traceable to the rich and powerful in this world," and not of God. "This new knowledge about themselves and the world, as disclosed in and through the resurrection, requires that the poor practise political activity against the social and economic structure that makes them poor. Not to fight is to deny the freedom of the resurrection."[6]

It is above all the humble of the earth who can cry, "No suffering is unimportant to God, for it is his suffering. No death is inconsequential to him because it is his death. And no life is not dear to him because it is his life. If this God is on our side, who can be against us?"[7]

"This simply means that the oppressed have a future not made with human hands."[8]

"In the end the Kingdom will come because sooner or later man will believe....

"Why? Because there is a God.

"....Anyone who thinks that evil will have the last word or that good and evil have a fifty-fifty chance is an atheist....

"Faith in the Kingdom of God, then, is not merely a matter of subscribing to the values of the Kingdom and vaguely hoping that it may one day come on earth. Faith in the Kingdom is the conviction that whatever else the Kingdom will come" (Nolan, South Africa).[9]

But it is both coming and growing now in history. For, "The Kingdom is not merely reflected, foreshadowed...in history, but actually present, operative ... however imperfectly and partially...."[10] "To hope in Christ is at the same time to believe in the adventure of history which opens infinite vistas to the love and action of the Christian."[11]

*"God kills death"* (Choan-Seng Song).[12] God's Kingdom is being established on earth. There is every hope for eternal life. Therefore the oppressed in their struggle for food and justice have no reason to despair.

"Usually when the reality of the political situation dawns upon the oppressed, those who have no vision from another world tend to give up in despair. But those who have heard about the coming of the Lord Jesus and have a vision of crossing on the other side of Jordan, are not terribly disturbed about what happens in Washington, D.C."[13]

The oppressed have no reason to fear. "The resurrection is a politics without fear. It conquers the fear of the cross and overpowers fear of darkness and death. Fear makes us morbid and inactive. It immobilizes us, drains something vital from us, and makes us less human. When we become captives of fear, we are likely to act and react solely on the basis of the instinct for survival and self-protection. Fear turns us into animals of instinct, corrupts human relationships, and destroys human integrity .... Resurrection sets us free from such fear and makes us free for what is truly human."[14]

*"A Christian has no self-image to preserve, no need to be justified by the blamelessness of his action.... The Christian can offer his praxis (actions) to the fire of criticism totally and unreservedly in the trust of free grace, just as he can offer his body totally and unreservedly in the hope of resurrection"* (Miguez Bonino, Argentina).[15] Christians can afford to take moral risks, to get their hands dirty. In the resurrection of Christ we are all assured of God's forgiveness and freed from the minutiae of the law. Even if, in a pressured situation, we are not absolutely certain that what we are doing is right, we

BECAUSE ·I· LIVE

YOU ALSO SHALL LIVE

can still, in love, act, trusting in God's forgiving grace.

*"As Spirit the resurrected Christ acts wherever he wishes"* (Boff).[16] The resurrection was God's way of making Jesus' support available to people of all time, and of releasing God's Spirit in the world. It can never be true, however, that the Church has a monopoly on that Spirit. Christians can never regard themselves as the spiritual "haves" and the rest of the world as the "have nots." "They (Christians) must recognize and rejoice in the fact that those outside are being saved, developed and liberated to the degree that they respond to the challenge of God in history. Their mission consists not so much in work for the liberation of others as in seeking liberation with others. They have as much to learn from others as others have to learn from them. The only thing they have and others do not, is their personal encounter with Jesus as mediating the presence of God" (Kappen, India).[17]

These are some thoughts of our Christian brothers and sisters in the Third World as they live out the cross and resurrection of our Lord. But throughout the history of the church, the pattern of suffering, death, renewal, and fresh life has been continually repeated. The traditions of the denominations are small corners of that fabric.

# III

CROSS AND RESURRECTION IN OUR HERITAGE

There is an open prison in one corner of the old Edinburgh graveyard. It's only a stone enclosure, and many of our Presbyterian grandparents chose to be interned there, exposed to the raw Scottish winters, rather than renounce their new Protestantism. Following Luther and Calvin, they stubbornly believed in:
- justification by grace through faith: we are made right with God not by our actions but only by trust in God's grace given through Jesus Christ
- the basic authority of the Bible over the church
- the "priesthood of all believers": all Christians can communicate directly with God, without the mediation of

priests, and all are responsible for each other's spiritual welfare.

Many of them died.

The Congregationalists came directly out of English Puritanism, a movement that stressed disciplined modest living, simple heartfelt worship, and, as with the Presbyterians, the main tenets of the Protestant reformation. What the Congregationalists added was the fierce independence of each congregation. Only the local congregation, not centralized authorities, could know what was spiritually best for its people. The Congregationalists, like the Presbyterians, were persecuted for many generations, though without the same extreme cruelty.

In the eighteenth century, John and Charles Wesley, George Whitefield and their followers preached their way up and down England in fields and in tents to the new, unchurched, and miserable industrial populations. They spoke with passion of how the love of Jesus could transform lives, and they wrote lusty new hymns to popular beer hall tunes. Their emphasis on being filled with the Spirit went with a strong concern for social justice. Wesley's encouragement of decentralized lay authority and participation laid the groundwork for an active, democratically minded working class. Large numbers of Methodists were involved in the beginnings of the British labour movement, to the extent that at times Methodism became more or less synonymous with sedition.[18]

The Evangelical United Brethren was a union of two German-speaking churches in North America: the United Brethren, which, like early Methodism, stressed personal conversion and small prayer groups, and the Evangelical Church, a reformed German church which believed in simple, informal worship, and effectively reached out to unchurched German speaking settlers.[19]

Presbyterian, Congregationalist, Methodist, Evangelical United Brethren, were all in their time new sparks in a dying or corrupt Christianity. These are the roots of The United Church of Canada. They were dissenting, non-conformist and "rabble-rousing." They emphasized dependence on the Spirit, modesty of life-style, simplicity in worship, and a concern for social justice. Other denominations could trace their heritage in similar ways.

## NEW SHOOTS

It is a fact of nature, however, that all new shoots with time become faded and tired. Sociologically, they gradually become absorbed into the dominant culture and are domesticated. The Church throughout its history has had a disturbing tendency to become a chaplaincy to the status quo, but it has also had a remarkable ability, just when it has looked very dead indeed, to put out new shoots, whether they be monasticism or Methodism. And as these have been absorbed into the world, new shoots have appeared. It is a tradition the Church has come by honestly, since Jesus himself was new wine in the old wineskins of first century Israel.

Few would disagree that the Church desperately needs fresh shoots at this moment. Statements like the following are far from uncommon in Christian and non-Christian writing:

"Today, practising Christians are a minority, and not only in Sweden or the Soviet Union. In all countries containing a majority of baptized Christians among their populations, actual believers and practisers constitute a minority and are predominantly defensive in attitude. Their social influence for the good is very small - they are more closely concerned with the protection of their inheritance" (Adolf Holl).[20]

What those present shoots might be in your situation you can best say. But there would seem to be a few obvious indications.

## OUR PERSONAL STORIES

Where along the way have we lost our ability to speak of our faith? Our non-conformist grandparents weren't similarly tongue-tied. When did it become in bad taste to discuss religion, except in the most abstract terms, and when did we become embarrassed by such a question as "What is God doing in your life?" Could we now even conceive of a "tent meeting" in the local shopping mall? Is the personal communication of our faith a skill which has atrophied through disuse? Does it reflect a lack of spirituality, as family prayers and Bible reading and personal devotions have gone out of vogue? How did we lose our strongly emotional, rabble-rousing roots? And, what is more pertinent, how can we learn to express our faith again openly and enthusiastically?

### BACK TO LIFE-STYLE AND GLOBAL JUSTICE

Few would disagree either that along the way we have become very "conformed to this world," or that, out there, just within our line of vision, is a large hurting world. If we go our comfortable way and ignore it, we shall surely lose our credibility and deserve to do so.

### LIFE NOT DEATH

Reading the words of many present-day writers alongside the words of Jesus, one hears a curious echoing effect. Jesus was speaking to a time of crisis: if you don't change, you will sooner or later destroy yourselves. But he was also crying out that precisely because of this crisis it was a unique time of opportunity. Our time, perhaps more than any time since his, is at a crisis point: ecological breakdown, overpopulation, spiraling violence, the structural oppression of North over South, First World over Third World, the overhanging threat of nuclear war. The question is, does the Church, the whole Church, have the flexibility to respond, to catch a new vision of what Jesus was about, and to put out new shoots? Is the Church prepared to be recklessly loving, take risks, look foolish? Are you and I prepared to make a straightforward commitment to the Kingdom?

Jesus offers us a way to life rather than a way of death, but only we can reach out and grasp it.

# FOOTNOTES
# AND REFERENCES

CHAPTER ONE

1 Jose Miguez-Bonino, *Doing Theology in a Revolutionary Situation,* Philadelphia, Fortress Press, 1975, p. 2.
2 Dietrich Bonhoeffer, *Letters and Papers from Prison,* (ed.) E. Bethge, (enlarged edition) London, S.C.M. Press, 1971, p. 360.
3 James Cone, *God of the Oppressed,* New York, Seabury, p. 115.
4 Leonardo Boff, *Jesus Christ Liberator,* A Critical Christology for Our Time, Maryknoll, Orbis, 1972, p. 11.

CHAPTER TWO

1 Albert Nolan, *Jesus Before Christianity,* London, Darton, Longman and Todd, p. 22f.
2 Herbert Danby, (Trans.)*The Mishnah,* (Hallah, 2, 3) Oxford, Clarendon Press, 1933, p. 84.
3 Louis Finkelstein, *The Pharisees,* Philadelphia, Jewish Publication Society of America, 1938, p. 13.
4 Louis Cassels, *This Fellow Jesus,* New York, Pyramid Publications, 1973, p. 64.
5 Jon Sobrino, "Who are the Poor?... Those Who Die," in *Signs of the Times,* ed. N. Vale, The United Church of Canada, 1981, p. 50.
6 Sebastian Kappen, *Jesus and Freedom,* Maryknoll, Orbis, 1977, p. 153.

CHAPTER THREE

1 The People's Mass of the Nicaraguans, quoted in *Mission Magazine,* The United Church of Canada, Vol. 5, No. 3, 1981, p. 20.
2 James H. Cone, *God of the Oppressed,* New York, Seabury Press, 1975, p. 135.
3 Jon Sobrino, "Who are the Poor?... Those Who Die," in *Signs of the Times,* (ed.) N. Vale, The United Church of Canada, 1981, p. 47.
4 Dr. Mark Warren of Nyadiri Methodist Hospital, Zimbabwe.
5 Cyril H. Powles, *Towards a Theology of Mission for Today,* Anglican Church of Canada, 1982, p. 2.
6 Steve Biko, "Black Consciousness and the Quest for a New Humanity," in *The Challenge of Black Theology in South Africa,* (ed.) Basil Moore, Atlanta, John Knox Press, 1973, p. 47.
7 George L. Brinkman, "Farm Incomes in Canada," Economic Council of Canada, Ottawa, 1981.
8 "The Working Poor: People and Programs, A Statistical Profile Prepared by the National Council of Welfare," Ottawa, March 1981, pp. 121f.
9 Patricia Clarke, "Our Responsibility: Be There and Be Heard," in *Observer,* The United Church of Canada, April 1982, p. 33.
10 E.F. Schumacher, "Implications of the Limits to Growth Debate - Small is Beautiful," in *Anticipation,* No. 13, Dec. 1972, World Council of Churches.
11 John Raines, "Middle America: Up Against the Wall and Going Nowhere," in *Christian Century,* May 2, 1973.
12 John V. Taylor, *Enough is Enough,* London, S.C.M. Press, 1975, p. 8.
13 Frances Moore Lappé, et al. "Barriers to Development," in *Signs of the Times,* p. 154.
14 Adam Daniel Finnerty, *No More Plastic Jesus, Global Justice and Christian Lifestyle,* Maryknoll, Orbis Books, 1979, p. 4.
15 Robert Carty and Virginia Smith, *Perpetuating Poverty, The Political Economy of Canadian Foreign Aid,* Toronto, Between the Lines, 1981, pp. 86f.
16 Frances Moore Lappé, *Diet for a Small Planet,* Friends of the Earth/Ballantine, New York, 1971, p. 6. Cf also Lappé, *Food First, Beyond the Myth of Scarcity,* Boston, Houghton-Mifflin, 1977.

[17] Doris J. Longacre, *Living More with Less,* Kitchener, Herald Press, 1980, p. 55.

[18] Derek Evans, Paper for British Columbia Conference of The United Church of Canada, 1980.

[19] Adam Daniel Corson-Finnerty, *World Citizen, Action for Global Justice,* Maryknoll, Orbis, 1982, p. 112.

## CHAPTER FOUR

[1] For a thorough account of the participation of women in one revolutionary struggle, see Margaret Randall, *Sandino's Daughters: Testimonies of Nicaraguan Women in Struggle,* Vancouver, New Star Books, 1981.

[2] Rosemary Radford Reuther, *New Woman, New Earth,* New York, Seabury Press, 1975, p. 30.

[3] Rosemary Reuther, Eleanor McLaughlin, *Women of Spirit,* New York, Simon and Schuster, 1979, p. 25.

[4] Cf. Louis Finkelstein, *Akiba, Scholar, Saint and Martyr,* New York, Atheneum, 1970, p. 190.

[5] Cf. Leonard Swidler, *Biblical Affirmations of Women,* Philadelphia, Westminster Press, 1979, p. 155.

[6] Cf. Swidler, *op. cit.,* p. 157.

[7] Cf. H. Danby, (ed.) *The Mishnah,* Oxford, Clarendon Press, 1933, p. 446.

[8] Leonard Swidler, "Jesus was a Feminist," in *Catholic World,* January 1971, pp. 177-181.

[9] Cf. Rachel Conrad Wahlberg, *Jesus According to a Woman,* New York, Paulist Press, 1975, p. 22.

[10] Swidler, "Jesus was a Feminist," *Catholic World,* Jan. 1971, p. 179.

[11] Elizabeth Schussler Fiorenza, "Interpreting Patriarchal Traditions," in *The Liberating Word,* (ed.) L.M. Russell, Philadelphia, Westminister Press, 1976, p. 44.

[12] Michele Landsberg, "Some Day We'll Pay for the Scandal of Female Slave Labor," in *Signs of the Times,* (ed.) N. Vale, Toronto, The United Church of Canada, 1981, p. 218.

[13] Fiorenza, *op. cit.,* p. 49.

[14] Wahlberg, *op. cit.,* p. 8.

[15] Reuther, *New Woman, New Earth,* p. 132.

## CHAPTER FIVE

[1] Joachim Jeremias, *New Testament Theology,* Part One,

London, SCM Press, 1971, p. 117; Albert Nolan, *Jesus Before Christianity,* London, Darton, Longman and Todd, 1977, p. 99.

2 Rosemary Radford Reuther, *Faith and Fratricide, The Theological Roots of Anti-Semitism,* New York, Seabury Press, 1979, pp. 64-115; D.R.A. Hare, *The Theme of Jewish Persecution of Christians in the Gospel According to Matthew,* Cambridge University Press, 1967.

3 E.P. Sanders, *Paul and Palestinian Judaism,* Philadelphia, Fortress Press, 1971, pp. 426-427.

4 *Ibid.,* pp. 147ff, pp. 422-427.

5 Josephus, *Antiquities,* 17, 2.

6 Jeremias, *op. cit.,* pp. 143-144.

7 Louis Finkelstein, *The Pharisees,* Philadelphia, Jewish Publication Society of America, 1938, p. xv.

8 Jeremias, *op. cit.,* pp. 76-77.

9 Hans Conzelmann, *Jesus,* Philadelphia, Fortress Press, 1973, pp. 33-34.

## CHAPTER SIX

1 Cf. Albert Nolan, *Jesus Before Christianity,* London, Longman, Darton and Todd, 1977, p. 93.

2 J. Jeremias, *New Testament Theology,* Part One, London, S.C.M. Press, 1971, p. 278.

3 Josephus, *Antiquities,* 18:55-57; cf. Nolan, *op.cit.,* p. 128.

4 Philo, *Legatio ad Gaium,* 299-305; cf. Nolan, *op. cit.,* p. 128.

5 Alan Richardson, *The Political Christ,* Philadelphia, Westminster Press, 1973, pp. 30-31.

6 Cf. S.G.F. Brandon, *Jesus and the Zealots,* Manchester University Press, 1967; for contrasting opinion, cf. A. Richardson, *op. cit.,* pp. 28f.

7 Jeremias, *op. cit.,* p. 279.

8 E. Trocmé, *Jesus and His Contemporaries,* London, S.C.M. Press, 1973, pp. 110-120.

9 Cf. Paul Winter, *On the Trial of Jesus,* Berlin, 1961.

10 Richardson, *op. cit.,* p. 7.

11 Helder Camara, *Spiral of Violence,* London, 1971, p. 30.

12 G. Vermes, *Jesus the Jew, a Historian's Reading of the Gospels,* London, 1973, p. 176.

13 Jeremias, *op. cit.,* pp. 287-288.

14 Harold Wells, "Raising Power Against the Power Structures,"

in *Journal of Theology for Southern Africa,* 30, March 1980, pp. 63-68.

## CHAPTER SEVEN

[1] Leonardo Boff, *Jesus Christ Liberator,* Maryknoll, Orbis Books, 1978, p. 129.

[2] Choan-Seng Song, *Third-Eye Theology,* Maryknoll, Orbis Books, 1979, p. 163.

[3] *Ibid.,* p. 167.

[4] *Ibid.,* p. 164.

[5] James Cone, *God of the Oppressed,* Seabury Press, New York, 1975, p. 125.

[6] *Ibid.*

[7] Choan-Seng Song, *op. cit.,* p. 166.

[8] Cone, *op. cit.,* p. 158.

[9] Albert Nolan, *Jesus Before Christianity,* London, Darton, Longman and Todd, 1977, p. 85.

[10] Jose Miguez Bonino, *Doing Theology in a Revolutionary Situation,* p. 142.

[11] Gustavo Gutierrez, *A Theology of Liberation,* London S.C.M. Press, 1973, p. 239.

[12] Choan-Seng Song, *op. cit.,* p. 164.

[13] Cone, *op. cit.,* p. 132.

[14] Choan-Seng Song, *op. cit.,* p. 253.

[15] Miguez Bonino, *op. cit.,* p. 100.

[16] Boff, *op. cit.,* p. 220.

[17] Sebastian Kappen, *Jesus and Freedom,* Maryknoll, Orbis Books, 1977, p. 152.

[18] Cf. J. Marlow, *The Tolpuddle Martyrs,* London, Andre Deutsch, 1971; and H. Pelling, *A History of British Trade Unionism,* London, Macmillan and Co., 1963, pp. 63, 74.

[19] J.H. Getz, (ed.) *A Century in Canada,* Evangelical United Brethren, Kitchener, 1964, pp. 5-6.

[20] Adolf Holl, *Jesus in Bad Company,* New York, Avon, 1971, p. 60.

# STUDY GUIDE

# SUGGESTIONS
# FOR GROUP MEETINGS

If you are interested in doing the study you might commit yourself to meet with a group once a week for seven weeks and to read a chapter each week before coming.

You may decide to meet in a church parlour or hall, minister's study, or perhaps (if the group is not too large) in someone's home. A family living room can prove to be the friendliest and warmest environment for this kind of event.

This study guide offers fairly detailed suggestions for each meeting. It's important, however, to be flexible about the program and to be aware of the group's needs. Some groups may enjoy a fairly busy session with a number of group activities and questions. Others may happily dig into one or two questions. Group leaders should feel free to use any, all, or none of the suggestions listed.

Often the most effective suggestions come from the group. The leader might, at the beginning of the meeting, ask what questions arose in people's minds as they read the text, list these, and use them as the basis for discussion in place of the questions we have proposed.

Generally, it's important that everyone feel welcome and accepted by the group, so that all will participate comfortably. Most people are more likely to express themselves openly in smaller rather than larger groups. Groups of five or six are usually optimum. A group of over ten should be split in two (or more) for part of the meeting.

Seating should be arranged preferably in a circle, both for

the group as a whole and for smaller buzz groups.

The leader will probably need to use a flip chart or blackboard. Participants should bring with them the study book and a Bible. It's also a good idea, if possible, to have one or two good Bible commentaries on hand.

Beverages might be available where people can help themselves.

For the final meeting, members might decide to include a simple pot luck supper or consider having supper before each meeting. (Start earlier so you don't eat into the discussion time.)

The sessions in this study guide have been structured as follows:
- opening prayer
- activities for the whole group. These help members of the group to know each other better and begin opening up the content of the chapter
- review: reading the summary of the chapter and Bible passages
- Track A OR B (there will not be time for both) for small group discussion. We have included two tracks of questions for those who prefer a particular emphasis:
  *Track A* directs the group's attention specifically to the text of *Jesus Means Life,* with reference to key biblical passages.
  *Track B* focusses closely on one or two biblical passages with reference back to the text of *Jesus Means Life.*
For some meetings, we have included a film suggestion and accompanying questions as an alternative around which the small group discussion can be built.
- feedback from small discussion groups to the whole group
- worship

We suggest meetings be one and a half to two hours, with about an hour for discussion of the tracks or film.

Note: All hymn references in the worship suggestions are from the Anglican-United Church Hymn Book.

# THE FIRST SESSION

PURPOSE:

1. To help members of the group get to know each other.
2. To appreciate the difficulties in knowing the real Jesus and to understand how *we* can know him.

OPENING PRAYER

Begin the session with prayer, asking that the Spirit of Jesus be among you and that God's Word and Truth may be heard.

ACTIVITY FOR THE WHOLE GROUP

## A. *Ice Breakers*

1. If the members do not know one another, the group might break into pairs. Each person interviews her or his partner and then all introduce their partners to the group for about one minute.

*or*

2. Go around the circle. Let each person introduce him or herself and then complete one of the following statements:

a. I've never been in a group like this before so I hope I...

b. What I liked best about another group I was in was...

*or*

3. Have each person in the group state her/his name and the group divide into pairs. The leader will then give them one of the following questions (or questions of your own choice) to discuss for two minutes. At the end of the two

minutes the group members change partners and are given another question. This can be repeated two or three more times.

    a. Why have you come to the group?

    b. Who (or what) has taught you most about Christian faith?

    c. In what ways do you think Jesus is important for our own times?

## B. Group Relations

Most participants will have been in other groups either in the church, the community or at work and will have some ideas about what made those groups function happily (or the reverse). Encourage them to draw upon their experience.

The group leader may have the following suggestions listed on the chart or board. A member of the group can read them out and the group be invited to comment, agree, disagree, and suggest additions.

1. *Be honest.* Say what you are really feeling and thinking and not what you think the group wants to hear. Don't be afraid to disagree with another viewpoint and don't be afraid to express feelings as well as thoughts.

2. *Listen to the other members.* Sometimes this may mean not expressing all your own ideas (even some of the really good ones).

3. *No one should dominate the conversation (especially the leader)!* Conversation time should be shared fairly around the group.

4. *Never laugh at or ridicule another member's opinions.*

5. *Agree to sometimes disagree.* Be aware that there is not always one right answer to the questions we are discussing and general agreement within the group may not be possible.

6. Your suggestions?

*or (better still)*

The group leader may offer one of the above as an example and then get further suggestions from the group.

REVIEW

Read the Bible passages: Luke 1: 1-4 and John 20: 30-31, and the summary below.

SUMMARY

The images we have of Jesus are very different, depending on when and where we live and our social circumstances. We may be tempted to create Jesus in our own image and use him for our own purposes, and the way we see him is from our own angle. This does not mean, however, that our images of him need be wildly distorted. We can still attempt to see him honestly and objectively.

A further complication in knowing Jesus is the way his life has been recorded. The gospels are collections of stories preserved by different people in different places and reflect the interests and enthusiasms of these communities and the individual gospel writers. The differences in the records and difficulty in knowing the historical truth have led some biblical scholars to question whether anything could be known for certain, and then whether anything *need* be known. Isn't it the Christ of faith who gives us life, not a historical figure?

These views have been strongly questioned by a group of scholars who maintain that certain facts about the historical Jesus are not in question. They point to the ability of ancient peoples to preserve large bodies of material accurately, and the stamp of a single great person which marks the material we have. Third World Christians, looking for a clear model for action, are also among those turning back for another look at the historical Jesus.

Finally, the appropriate way to know Jesus is as a person. Although the views of other Christians past and present must inform and correct our view of him, in the end we respond to him as a person or not at all.

SMALL GROUP DISCUSSION

*Track A*

Divide into small groups and discuss some or all of the

following questions.

1. "We must see him from some perspective and that can only be our own."

a. The Sunday school in which we grew up always began with the room darkened and a slide of the Sallman head of Christ projected on the screen. There were a few seconds of silence and then we sang softly "Turn Your Eyes Upon Jesus." Many of us grew up loving that picture. It portrays a very handsome young man with spiritually intense eyes, a "Fairest Lord Jesus." It is probably the most popular religious picture of Jesus among the Protestant churches. Why? What is there in it that is so appealing to us?

b. The People's Mass of Nicaragua speaks of "the God of the worn and leathery face, the God who sweats in the street." Why is this image so beloved in Nicaragua? Nicaragua has just been through a violent revolution. How would you expect the Sallman Jesus to react in that situation? How would you expect the Jesus of the People's Mass to react? Is it possible to say which image is truer to the gospel records?

2. "Are the gospels really reliable records of the events?"

a. The memories we have and cherish of certain events are very different. Think yourself into this situation:

You have just been married. A number of people are giving their descriptions of and reactions to the wedding. What are some of the things these people might say? (Think about this or choose three different members of the group to play these parts.)

- a friend of the family (her flowers were lovely...)
- the minister (I wish a crowd like that would come on Sunday...)
- you (I was in such a daze I hardly knew what was happening...)

Although their views are different, one is not necessarily more accurate than the others.

b. A teenager you know is disturbed because he or she has just been hit by the differences in the gospel records (possibly after comparing the four accounts of the resurrection). Using (a) as an example and ideas from the text, p. 3 imagine you are explaining to him or her why these differences exist. Again you might act this out with two members of the group.

3. "We respond to him as a person or not at all." If you meet someone you want to know better, what do you do? Is there any similarity between this and how you get to know Jesus? Do you regard Jesus as a person, or is he primarily a historical figure or an idea? What are the ways in which you have come to know him or know of him?

*Track B*

Read again Luke 1: 1-4.

Divide into small groups and use some or all of these questions.

1. Why did Luke decide to write his gospel? On what was he basing it?

2. Are there some reasons why the gospels were *not* written by the eyewitnesses but by those who heard their stories?

3. Why were a number of different accounts of the story of Jesus written (See the text, p. 3)?

Read again John 20: 30-31.

4. How did John's purpose differ from Luke's purpose?

5. Consider how their different purposes led them to write quite different kinds of gospels (See the text, p. 4).

6. John writes "so that you might believe that Jesus is the Christ." Has he achieved his purpose? Do *you* find the stories of John and his fellow writers convincing? Why or why not?

7. Consider a few ways in which Jesus gives us life.

FEEDBACK

If the group has been divided, it can come back together and share what has been said in the small groups for about ten minutes.

WORSHIP

*A Hymn*

from *The Hymn Book* may be sung (if the group wishes) - perhaps No. 65 (Jesus where'er thy people meet) or No. 343 (Jesus thou joy of loving hearts).

*Prayer in the Group*

We suggest that during the sessions all members of the group have the opportunity to lead in prayer (though they should not be pressured to do so if they are uncomfortable with it). The prayers might reflect what has gone on in the meeting and express other personal concerns members may have. If the leader asks beforehand for prayer suggestions, members can then more easily pray for each other's concerns.

You may sometimes use a bidding prayer, in which one member directs the group to a particular concern (e.g., let us pray for our brothers and sisters in the world who are unjustly imprisoned). There is then a period of silence and another direction, (let us...) followed by another silence, and so on.

*Prayer for this Session*

The leader or other members may offer prayer for

- the courage and honesty to see Jesus as clearly as possible
- generosity to accept and sympathize with other people's views of him
- the grace to see other Christians, whatever their nationalities, denominations or viewpoints, as one family
- the gift of the Spirit of Jesus, so that each may come to know him in a personal way
- particular people in the local church or community who are ill, or in any kind of trouble or distress.

Close with the Lord's Prayer in unison.

ALTERNATIVE PROGRAM

The filmstrip *Who Do YOU Say That I Am?* shows how Jesus has been seen through the eyes of artists in different times and places. Painters like Rembrandt and Kurelek, artists from India, Burma, and North America portray their understanding of the life and work of Jesus.

*Who Do YOU Say That I Am?* comes with a cassette and

user's guide. It would form a good basis of discussion for this session. Order from AVEL. (See Appendix X for AVEL addresses.)

# THE SECOND SESSION

PURPOSE:

To understand the ways in which Jesus brought life to the poor of his day.

OPENING PRAYER

ACTIVITY FOR THE WHOLE GROUP

The group might begin by taking a memory trip together. The leader or one of the members might read the suggestions below for recalling our memories of Jesus. These should be read slowly with sufficient pauses, so that people have time to think back. Group members should be asked to close their eyes for better concentration.

- what are your earliest memories of Jesus? Perhaps a parent, grandparent or other adult is talking to you about him. What is his or her tone of voice?
- you are a small child saying your bedtime prayers. What picture of Jesus comes into your mind?
- you are in Sunday school. What pictures did you have there of Jesus? What hymns did you sing about him? What words were most often used to describe him? How did you feel about Jesus?
- you are in a youth group or confirmation class. How are your ideas about Jesus changing? Do you have any serious questions about him?
- you are an adult in church. How does your congregation primarily think of Jesus? Can you recall an adult ex-

perience you've had that has changed your way of looking at Jesus?
- you are in this study group. What were your feelings about Jesus as you read this chapter?
- if Jesus were to walk in the door now what would he be like? How would you describe his face? How is he dressed? What kind of vehicle did he arrive in? How would he talk to you and the others in the room?
Do you think you would enjoy his company?
Observe about a minute of silence for meditation.

REVIEW:

Read the Bible passages: Luke 4:18-19, Matt. 11: 28-30 and John 2:1-11, and the summary below.

SUMMARY

For many Christians in the world today, the central fact about Jesus is that he was poor. He was poor because he chose to be poor and associate with the poor. His family were probably relatively prosperous tradespeople, and he was educated in the synagogue school. As the gospels tell it, he could only have made this peculiar choice out of an extravagant, reckless compassion.

The majority of the population in Jesus' day were either economically poor to a degree that we can barely imagine, or so-called sinners, groups of people who couldn't or didn't keep the law. It was to these two groups that Jesus decided he had been sent, and what he promised them was life in all its fullness. This he gave in basically three ways:
- he healed them: he created in them a faith that was able to change impossible circumstances
- he lived with them, eating and drinking with them, accepting them, defending them
- he promised them the Kingdom of God: he convinced them that God's rule was being established on earth and that in this new order they would have an honoured place. He gave them hope.

SMALL GROUP DISCUSSION

*Track A*

1. "Jesus himself saw his work as healing the sick..." Are the healing miracles of Jesus believable to you? Do you have any personal experiences of healing miracles? If so, you might share some of these within the group.

2. "They called him a glutton and a drunkard."

a. Jesus was a party goer and often pictures the Kingdom of God in terms of a party (e.g. Luke 14:16), but Christians generally have a reputation for being more than average serious and sober. Why?

b. How was it that Jesus could be lighthearted in the midst of what he considered an urgent mission?

c. Or are we misinterpreting the facts? Was he really at the parties to convert people?

d. Is Jesus here putting a large blessing on hospitality? One writer in the book *Living More with Less* (p. 254) says "For me the statement 'I wanted to have you over but I've just been too busy' not only reflects bad habits and bad manners but immoral values." Is this true? Do we tend to neglect simple hospitality? If so, why?

3. We say "You are known by the company you keep" and imply that we should be careful about the people we associate with or we'll endanger our reputation. But Jesus kept the worst sort of company and had, in some quarters, an exceedingly bad reputation.

a. Could it be that as followers of his we are too selective and limited in our friends and associates? If yes, why?

b. In what ways do you (and your group) stand in solidarity with the poor and sinners in your community, the nation, the world?

c. In what other ways might you do this?

4. "There is more than one way of being bent."

a. Are there ways in which you consider yourself poor (See the text, p. 13)?

5. "The Kingdom of God is like a mustard seed."

a. Where have you seen signs of God's Kingdom grow-

ing in the past year:
- in your church
- in your community
- in the nation
- in the world?

b. Where do you see the Kingdom developing in history?

c. There is a saying:

"If it's to be
It must be done
By me."

To what extent is this true of the Kingdom of God?

*Track B*

In connection with some of the Bible study questions, we will ask you to read selections from *The Gospel in Solentiname,* found in the Appendix. We have included passages from this book so that you will have the participation of a few of the Third World's poor in your discussion. Solentiname is a remote series of islands in Nicaragua; the passages are from Bible studies by very poor and often illiterate peasants. They were taped and written down by Father Ernesto Cardenal. We hope you will listen carefully to what these people are saying, but also feel free to argue with them.

Many of these people were killed in raids by Somozan soldiers before the Nicaraguan revolution.

Use one or two of the following:

Read Luke 4:18-19.

1. Jesus is quoting the Messianic prophecy of Isaiah 61 and referring it to himself. Why did he quote Isaiah? Why not just say "I'm the Messiah"?

2. What kind of Messiah was Jesus proclaiming himself to be?

3. This passage has often been interpreted as referring only to the spiritually poor, captive, blind, and oppressed. But Jesus' constant concern was with the economically poor and the real blind. Why, then, do we spiritualize the text?

Read Matthew 11:28-30.

1. How did Jesus give rest to those who laboured and were heavy laden in his day (See the text, p. 15)?
2. Who are those "who labour and are heavy laden" today?
3. How does Jesus give them rest?
Read *Solentiname,* Appendix II.
4. According to the peasants of Solentiname, who is Jesus calling here ("Come unto me...")?
5. What is the comfort he offers them?
6. Compare these views with your own answers to questions 2 and 3.
Read John 2:1-11.
1. Why did Jesus perform his first miracle, according to John, at a wedding feast?
2. Why did Jesus go to parties?
3. Wine often has a symbolic meaning. What do you think it means here?
Read *Solentiname* in Appendix I.
4. What significance does the wine have to the peasants of Solentiname? (Compare this with your answer to number 3 above.)
5. Why do the peasants of Solentiname think Jesus will be drinking wine with them in the Kingdom of Heaven?
6. They often distinguish between good parties and drunken brawls. Why will the Kingdom be like a good party?

FEEDBACK

WORSHIP

*A Hymn*
perhaps No. 278 (Thy kingdom come) or
No. 298 (A workman in a village home)
*A Bidding Prayer*
The group leader may ask the people to pray in silence, directing their prayers along the following lines, leaving sufficient pauses:

Let us thank God for gifts of healing. For healing our bodies, our emotions, our relationships
Let us thank God for seeking us out and for God's presence in other people
Let us thank God for building the Kingdom on earth and for the privilege of being part of it
Let us remember before God the poor of our own communities and nation
Let us remember "the bent ones" who are our sisters and brothers in other parts of the world:
- those without access to medical care
- those without adequate food, shelter and clothing
In remembering them we commit ourselves again to help and serve them in whatever ways we can, for Jesus' sake.

The Lord's Prayer, in unison.

# THE THIRD SESSION

PURPOSE:

1. To understand how Jesus continues to be with the poor and to give them life.
2. To consider some ways we can also be with them.

OPENING PRAYER

ACTIVITY FOR THE WHOLE GROUP

(If the group is larger than twenty, it would be preferable to break up into two or three groups.)

   1. Someone might read aloud the following passage from Adam Finnerty's book *No More Plastic Jesus:*

"A far more realistic image of our embattled planet might be that of an ocean liner, rather than a lifeboat. This ocean liner, too, is in danger of sinking, but not so much because of the hordes of hungry passengers clinging to the rail and massed together in its dirty and dangerous holds as because of the deportment of the first-class passengers. These passengers, making up about twenty-eight percent of the ship's list, have insisted on bringing along their automobiles, their freezers, their television sets, their kitchen disposal units, and their pets" (p. 2).

Assuming that we are among the first-class passengers, go around the room and have each person

   a. Name one thing they could not do without (apart from basic necessities).
   b. Name one thing they might consider giving up.

c. Name one thing they could give up easily.

2. All change is built on visions. Dream for a few minutes about the world as you would like to see it. Go around the group and have each member say what one thing they would most like to change in the world.

REVIEW:

Read the Bible passages: Amos 5:21-24 and Luke 12:15, and the summary below.

SUMMARY

Many of the poor today identify with Jesus as "the humble God" who like them suffers and dies. Jesus does for them now what he did then:

- he heals them: consider church medical facilities spread throughout the world, and the resurgence of spiritual healing in his name
- he promises them the Kingdom and challenges them to struggle for it now: out of the certain belief that Jesus wills their liberation and that his Kingdom will certainly come, there is a new emphasis in Third World countries on "doing the gospel" even at great personal risk.

As followers of Jesus, we need to make his concerns our own. There are people in our own country living in difficult circumstances: e.g., small farmers and single parents with small incomes. Within our own national community, compassion and justice as well as informed self-interest can only dictate a fairer distribution of income, and a wiser use of resources, particularly human resources, and better governmental and personal support systems. How we are implicated in Third World poverty is far from self-evident, but through imports, exports, investments, and development aid, Canadians are involved. Are we then responsible? Is there anything personally we can do?

Many Christians today in North America and Europe are involved in simplifying their life-style and in the global justice movement. The two must go together. If we are involved in justice issues but continue to live at the same standard, we

will not be taken seriously. But life-style change will have little or no immediate effect on global poverty and injustice.
The practical, politically informed steps we take as groups
will have the greatest impact.

The job is vast, but as Jesus points out, "inasmuch as you
have done it to one of the least of these, you have done it to
me."

SMALL GROUP DISCUSSION

*Track A*

1. "The history and reputation of missions is a very stained
garment."

"Through our mission givings they (church leaders)
direct carefully chosen and well monitored development
projects throughout the world."

Our next door neighbours at an African university were
black historians who felt they had been patronized and
domineered in missionary boarding schools. When we arrived on campus, the woman came over to announce,
"We hate missionaries."

But in the classrooms, some students would state flatly,
"Since the departure of large numbers of missionaries
and the colonial administration, the country has become
more and more corrupt and disorderly. Missionaries are a
blessing from God."

Whatever the viewpoint, the missionary issue was
always emotional. What would be some of the underlying
reasons for this (See the text, p. 25)?

2. "Justice and compassion can only dictate a fairer
distribution of income..."

Outline what might be some long term solutions to the
problems of the farmers and the single working mother
(pp. 28, 29).

3. "But if we are implicated, are we then responsible?"

a. Do you feel any responsibility for the Third World's
poor? Why or why not?

b. Do you think there are realistic solutions to the problem of world poverty and injustice? If so, discuss in

concrete terms what some of these might be.

4. "It may be that the most underused resources in the problem of global justice are our personal emotions and our human brains." The 1982 campaign against nuclear arms was a good example of how the public can be educated and mobilized on a given issue. It is an issue on which many groups are still working.

a. If you were or are involved in this movement you might discuss some of the things that were and are being done.

b. Is it possible for similar programs to be launched in regard to other major problems?

c. If you have been involved in other local or international groups that worked effectively for social change you might share your experience here.

5. "We build the Kingdom more effectively together." We might use Moses and the people of Israel as a working model for social change. Out of the conviction that God willed their liberation, they - *as a group questioned* the social conditions around them and saw that they didn't *have* to be like that - they planned, built an escape route, and *moved* out of those conditions - they established themselves in a new land, learned to use their self-government, made the change permanent.

How might you use this model for change - questioning, moving, establishing, together - in one of the following situations (or use your own example)? Give specific suggestions for what could be done.

a. The school board is drastically cutting back on classes for children with learning disabilities.

b. Good farm land is being rapidly used up by urban development.

c. The government announces that it supports elections in a Central American country, even though none of the major dissenting or protesting groups is permitted to participate.

*Track B*
Read again Amos 5:21-24.

1. Amos is telling the people of his day that religious rituals, music and singing are worse than useless unless "justice rolls down like waters..." Is justice for the poor the high priority of your local congregation? If not, what is? Are we locked into structures and/or rituals that require other priorities?

Read again Luke 12:15.

2. To what extent do we evaluate people's lives by the abundance of their possessions? To what extent is social status related to prosperity?

3. Why does Jesus warn us against an overevaluation of material possessions?

Read *Solentiname,* Appendix III.

4. For the people of Solentiname, on what does life depend?

5. They speak of riches that are shared *unevenly* as a curse. What reasons do they give for this?

6. Discuss concrete ways in which you might work toward a world in which economic goods are shared more evenly (See the text, p. 35).


ALTERNATIVE PROGRAM

In place of Track A or B use the film *Seeds of Health.* Filmstrips and slides recommended in this study guide can be obtained from United Church of Canada AVEL outlets. For addresses, see Appendix X.

Questions for discussion following the film:

N.B. Please read through the questions before viewing the film.

1. "They'll continue to be sick until they can solve this land tenure problem."

Discuss why this is so. See also the text, p. 36.

2. "They have little room to manoeuvre, but this doesn't stop them." What was the spark (or sparks) which motivated these people to start changing their situation?

3. This project only gave help to groups and not individuals. Why?

4. This project is partly financed by Canadian church funds. How is it "a well thought out leg up and not a strings attached handout?"

5. The film says, "Wherever the people have the courage to crucify greed and individualism there is resurrection." How could this be true of us?


FEEDBACK

WORSHIP

*A Hymn*
No. 210 (For the healing of the nations) or
No. 274  (Let there be light)
or (Face of a poor God) Appendix VI.
*Responsive Reading:*
Divide the whole group in two and have them read the following responsively. Have them read it through in silence first.

| *Group One* | *Group Two* |
|---|---|
| To have less<br>Is to be richer | It's richer to have less? |
| To need less<br>Is to be freer | But we enjoy our small luxuries |
| Enough is enough | But why settle for less<br>When you can have more? |
| Simplicity is beautiful<br>Clutter is crude | We worked hard<br>For what we've got |
| But if anyone has the world's goods and sees his brother in need, yet closes his heart against him, how does God's love abide in him (John 3:17)? | Yes, but some people are lazy. And God helps those who help themselves. The Bible also says "If anyone will not work let him not eat" (II Thess. 3:10). |
| We know how you feel, but Jesus said, "I was hungry and you fed me, I was thirsty and you gave me drink" | In this country we've been blessed with great abundance. We should thank God for all we have been given. |

Naked and you clothed me
In prison and you visited me

Don't make us feel guilty.
We need to feel OK.

Inasmuch as you have done
it to one of the least of these
you have done it to me

We'd like to agree. But you
can't change the world

It's difficult. "We're not
contending against flesh
and blood, but against the
principalities, against the
powers, against the world
rulers of this present
darkness..."

The world's a rotten place.
That's why the rich get
richer, and the poor get
poorer.

They don't have to. Justice
could roll down like waters,
and righteousness like an
everflowing stream.

Look, we'd like to see the
world a better place, but it's
hard to believe it will happen.

*Male Voices:* Faith is the substance of things hoped for, the
evidence of things not seen
*Female Voices:* Hope is the very climate of the human spirit,
the air it breathes in order to live. To lose hope is to die.
*All:* I have come that you might have life and have it in all its
fullness.

*Prayer*
Members may lead the whole group in prayer, thinking about
our own kinds of poverty, expressing concern especially for
those poor of our society and of the world.
*or*
Silence may be kept for a few minutes during which members
may pray or meditate on what has been said during the
meeting.
Close with the benediction in unison, standing with clasped
hands in a circle:

"The grace of our Lord Jesus Christ, and the love of God and the
fellowship of the Holy Spirit be with us all. Amen."

# THE FOURTH SESSION

PURPOSE

1. To explore how Jesus gave new life to women of his time.
2. To see what this implies for women and men today.

OPENING PRAYER

ACTIVITY FOR THE WHOLE GROUP

*Role Plays*
Choose one of the following to be spontaneously acted out, either by two people before the whole group, or divide into pairs and let each pair act out one of these situations. If there are not equal numbers of men and women, one partner can play the part of the woman and the other partner the man.

a. A couple discusses "Who is responsible for the rotten onion at the bottom of the fridge?" Assume that both partners have jobs outside the home.

b. In *First of All Persons,* Elizabeth Steel Genne and William H. Genne tell the following story: "We were riding in a car with a married couple. She expressed a desire for a wall hanging that she thought was beautiful. His reply was, 'If it were your own money you wanted to use on that sort of junk, it would be all right, but since it's my money, you can forget it' " (p. 26). Act out the exchange that followed.

c. A woman has just been offered a very good job in another city. Her husband is reluctant to leave his job. Discuss the situation.

REVIEW:

Read the Bible passages: Luke 8:43-48 and John 20:11-16, and the summary below.

## SUMMARY

Because of their second class status, their lack of control over their lives and lack of opportunity for development, women in many parts of the world can be numbered among the poor. The women of Jesus' time were poor in much the same way.

Jesus, against the background of his times, can only be thought of as radical in his treatment of women. He talked and argued with them openly, as in the passage about the Samaritan woman at the well and the Canaanite woman with the sick child. He defended "the sinner" from the city, who poured ointment on him, and the woman taken in adultery. He chose them as followers (see the stories of Mary and Martha) and he appeared first to them after the resurrection, making them his first witnesses. Through the centuries, however, we may have lost sight of the women of the gospels as whole persons and so have probably failed to see them as Jesus did.

For the last twenty years, the liberation of women in our society has become a conscious issue at a grassroots level. Besides making changes in how men and women see themselves and relate to each other, the issue has meant a general questioning of the unequal laws and working conditions women suffer under. It has also meant a questioning of the male hierarchy, of sexist language and male interpretations of scripture within the church. If we are honest, this movement should result, too, in a more critical awareness of ourselves, and increase our ability to see that we are all, in different circumstances, sometimes the oppressed and sometimes the oppressor.

Before both women and men today, there is a whole new set of options. It is a situation about which Jesus would have rejoiced.

SMALL GROUP DISCUSSION

*Track A*

1. The people who took part in the role plays might discuss how they felt as they were acting, — defensive, aggressive? Is this indicative of how women and men feel about each other in our society?

2. In a classroom for retraining women for non-traditional (hard hat) occupations at Sheridan College, Oakville, Ontario, there is a poster of a turtle with its head and feet pulled in. The caption reads, "NO GUTS NO GLORY." Assuming that glory means recognition, consider the following:

   a. Are women lacking recognition?

   b. If so, to what extent do you think it is because they have lacked initiative (guts)?

3. Consider the story of the woman who had a flow of blood for twelve years, and so was regarded as unclean and untouchable (Luke 8:43-48).

Look at it from *her point of view.*

   a. What types of suffering must this condition have entailed?

   b. Would there be any reason why she'd try to touch him in a crowd?

   c. How did she react when Jesus asked who had touched him?

   d. Since he must have known her embarrassment and he wasn't normally unfeeling, why did Jesus deliberately draw attention to her?

*Track B*

Read Luke 8:43-48.

   1. Consider Question 3 of Track A above.

   Read John 20:11-16.

   2. According to the accounts of the resurrection in all four of the gospels, Jesus revealed himself first to his women followers and used them as his first witnesses. Why?

3. What reasons might there be for Mary's being slow to recognize Jesus?

4. What does this passage reveal about the feelings of both Mary and Jesus?

Read Luke 24:10-11.

5. Why did the men think the women's witness was an "idle tale?"

ALTERNATIVE PROGRAM

As an alternative to Track A or B you may decide to use "Christian Women Around the World," a slide and tape presentation by Lois Wilson. Read the questions below before watching the slides.

1. List some of the outstanding qualities of women in the slides.

2. In what ways are these women successors (and imitators) of the women followers of Jesus?

3. a. Women have usually been excluded from leadership roles in the church. Why is it then that at a grassroots level they are often the main supporters of the church, and, like the women in these pictures, initiators of helping programs?

b. Why was it the women of Jesus' day responded so enthusiastically to his movement?

4. Is it easier in some ways for women than men to "opt for the poor?" If so, why?

FEEDBACK

WORSHIP

*A Hymn*
No. 282 (I feel the winds of God today) or
No. 177 (Sing we a song of high revolt)
*Prayer:*
The leader may ask the group what prayer concerns they have. The leader can invite group members to pray for each other's concerns in the few minutes that follow.
You might conclude with this prayer:

God our Parent
Who cares for us with the loving protectiveness of a mother
and the tender concern of a father
Give us courage that
Where there is injustice we may struggle for justice
Where there is inequality, equality
Where there is hurt, healing
Where there is despair, hope,
Where there is indifference, concern
Where there is complacency, a vision of your Kingdom.
God, grant that we may not seek so much to be comfortable
in your world,
As to see that all people are cared for,
That we may not strive so much to maintain our
rights and privileges
As to see that what is right is done and privilege is abolished.
Remind us that it is in extravagant loving that we are your children
And that it is in doing justice that your Kingdom comes.

Let the following benediction be said in unison

The blessing of the God of Sarah, as of Abraham;
the blessing of the Son, born of the Virgin Mary;
the blessing of the Holy Spirit, who broods over
us as a mother, her children. Amen*


*The Very Reverend Lois Wilson at her installation as Moderator
of The United Church of Canada, August, 1980.

# THE FIFTH SESSION

PURPOSE:

1. To understand how Jesus offered life to the respectable and religious people of his time.
2. To understand, by implication, how he offers life to "good" church people today.

OPENING PRAYER

ACTIVITY FOR THE WHOLE GROUP

Divide into pairs and, for between five and ten minutes, tell each other about one genuinely good person you have known. Did you also consider this person to be great? Then come together in the whole group for a few minutes and share some of your thoughts on what real goodness is.

REVIEW:

Read the Bible passages: Ephesians 2: 8-9 and Matthew 7: 1-5, and the summary below.

SUMMARY

In the gospels, a number of the good and respectable people of Jesus' day form a sub-plot which gradually gathers momentum and finally ends in tragedy. It would seem not that Jesus excluded these people from his movement, but that they excluded themselves, a sobering thought for those of us who may be numbered among the good and respectable in our own societies.

Jesus clashed with a number of groups in his society, but during his ministry his main opponents appear to have been some of the Pharisees. His criticisms of them were specific.

According to Jesus, these Pharisees commented at length and with hostility on much of what he said and did. They judged, and like the elder brother in the parable of the prodigal son, they wouldn't consider coming into the feast. They loved money, and he accused them of rapacity and greed. They badly wanted social status, whereas Jesus argued the greatest must be "the least of all." Because of their strict adherence to the law, they felt they had God's approval and despised those who were not similarly righteous. They oppressed the poor, losing sight of the fact that "God desires mercy and not sacrifice." They wanted spectacular miracles from Jesus so that they would know whether he was the Messiah. When these weren't forthcoming, they rejected the possibility that God's Spirit could be working in him.

What is clear from the gospels is that, even though he was never reconciled to these people he kept reaching out to them.

The disciples provide an interesting comparison with the above group. They, too, often failed to understand what Jesus was about, but what they had was faith in him and, in the end, it was the one thing needed.


SMALL GROUP DISCUSSION

*Track A*
Take a closer look at some of Jesus' main criticisms of these Pharisees and relate them to yourself.

1. "They talk too much."
Why do we talk too much, gossip, judge, belittle? Why were certain Pharisees so critical of Jesus? (Look at pages 66 and 67).
2. "They loved money."
One woman, after reading the first draft of this book, commented, "I'm left with the feeling that unless you're poor you don't rate as a Christian." But another man

flatly stated, "You've left too many loopholes. As a Christian with only one cottage and one house, I feel positively virtuous." How do we decide how many possessions we can have and still be a Christian? Is it mainly a matter of conscience, of what people around us have, or what? Can you set a few guidelines for how much is enough?

3. "They blew their own trumpets."

A journalist in our Bible study group told us of writing a story about a Catholic brother who personally collects left-over food from restaurants and bakeries every day and feeds large numbers of homeless men. But he doesn't let them talk during the meal. When she questioned him about this he explained, "If you listen to our average conversation, most of it is about how superior the speakers (or those connected to them) are. These men have nothing to brag about, so they fight. It's better if they keep quiet."

Is this a fair evaluation of our conversations? If we were really humble as Jesus commands, how might our conversations be different?

4. "They trusted too much in their own righteousness."

   a. It's a common experience among ministers that people like the morally athletic, the "pull-up-your-socks-and-improve" sermons better than sermons about the free love of God. Why?

   Could it be that we like to earn what we get?

   b. Martin Luther had a very different experience. After agonizing over his sins and his ability to even recall his sins (and in frustration throwing an ink pot at the devil), he was enormously and wonderfully relieved to realize from reading Romans that God's love and forgiveness is free and cannot be earned. Have you ever felt overwhelmed by the love and forgiveness of God? If so, you might share some of these experiences among the group.

5. "They asked for a sign."

Jesus' critics weren't content with the signs they saw. They wanted something more spectacular. In what ways do we expect God to perform to our specifications? Do we tend to look for God only in specified places and people? In your day to day living where do you most often find God?

6. "...even if their faith did at times falter, it was the one thing needed."

The outstanding characteristic of the disciples was their faith. Most of us would reject Mark Twain's definition that faith is believing things you know aren't true. But what *is* faith?

- a leap into the dark (making a decision before all the evidence is in)?
- a leap into the light (taking a risk on a good bet)?
- believing in the Bible and the doctrines of the church?
- trust in a person?
- holding hard to the conviction that life (and God) is finally good?
- or...?

*Track B*

Read again Ephesians 2: 8-9.

1. What does it mean to be "saved?" Is being saved different from having life in the sense that Jesus gives life?

2. The writer of Ephesians says that faith is a gift of God, which we have only to reach out and accept. But we also speak of growing in faith. What are some of the ways we do this?

Read Matthew 7: 1-5.

3. Jesus was very critical of certain Pharisees, yet he cautioned us against judging. Can we avoid judging others if we honestly think they are doing wrong? Is it possible to be critical and not judge?

4. Read *Solentiname* in Appendix IV.

a. According to Oscar, why do we judge other people?

b. These Christians of Solentiname decide the passage is "an important call to self-criticism." Do you agree?

c. How do they, in the final part of their discussion, live out the commandment not to judge?

FEEDBACK IN THE WHOLE GROUP

WORSHIP

*A Hymn*

No. 106 (Lord of the dance) or No. 79 (Rock of ages)

A member of the group may lead the rest in a prayer of confession, making the following suggestions, and leaving sufficient time for silent meditation and prayer.

- let us confess the times when we have spoken unkindly of others
- let us confess our over-attachment to material possessions
- let us confess that we are often too concerned with people thinking well of us
- let us confess that we tend to be self-satisfied, and forget the free loving grace of God
- let us thank God that through Jesus Christ he forgives us more than we deserve.

Stand in a circle with clasped hands and let one person lead in the following prayer:

Lord, we believe; help our unbelief.
Remind us of who we are,
the community of the faithful,
even with all our jabbering,
nit-picking, love of convenience
and self-satisfaction.

"Break our unnecessary and misplaced rigidities,
Break the dams behind which our energies puddle,
Break our castle walls and let the people in."*
Or at least bend us
to your will
And keep us in your grace.

Close by saying the benediction to each other:

"The grace of our Lord Jesus Christ,
The Love of God

*Wm E. Gibson, *A Covenant Group for Lifestyle Assessment,* New York, the United Presbyterian Church, 1978, p. 73.

And the fellowship of the Holy Spirit
Be with us all
Amen.''


FOR FURTHER STUDY

This chapter could very well lead to a desire to know more
about Judaism and our Jewish neighbours. You might like to
set up a dialogue group with Jewish people, scholars within
your community. Such a group could deal with the relationship between Jewish and early Christian communities, how
Judaism was practised during the era in which Jesus lived,
and the theological issues about which Jewish and Christian
people agree or differ. Such a dialogue group could be an
enriching experience.

# THE SIXTH SESSION

PURPOSE

1. To consider Jesus' relationship to the political structures of his society and how that relationship led to his death.
2. To consider the implications of his political attitude for us.

OPENING PRAYER

ACTIVITY FOR THE WHOLE GROUP

*A Chancel Drama*
Read together the following short play. A few suggestions have been added in case you wish to use it as part of a church service. In a service the lines do not necessarily need to be memorized, but can be well read.

### THERE WASN'T MUCH I COULD DO
*At the front of the church, five men are seated around the back and sides of a table. There are two coffee mugs on the table. One of the men, Jonah, gets up from the table and walks down into the congregation. He speaks as convincingly as possible.*

*Jonah:* You don't know me. The name's Jonah. I was a Sadducee at the time of Jesus of Nazareth. Sadducee may not mean much to you, but then it signified wealth, power, prestige. We were the aristrocracy, the government, the religious hierarchy.

  I sat on the Sanhedrin, the court that tried Jesus. A rather shady business, I thought. You see I liked the man. He had an uncanny way of pulling out the heart of the problem, and as charmed a tongue as you've ever heard. When he talked about God he convinced you he *knew*. Enthusiasm is a thin word for it. I thought he was probably a prophet, but I abstained in the final vote. I still feel bad about that. Quite frankly though, there wasn't much I could do. There were a few of us sympathetic, but we were outnumbered and there was really very little point in trying to defend him. Outvoted we'd still have to live with our fellow members. No one wants to see their family disgraced and ridiculed, even endangered. And it wasn't as if you could defend his behaviour. He didn't *have* to antagonize those Pharisees, and creating that scene in the temple was sheer madness. I mean, it wasn't as if it solved anything. I fully agree the temple trade was corrupt, but that was just a stupid gesture. After it there was no turning a blind eye to him.

If you have a few minutes, let me tell you about that last meeting of the Sanhedrin and I'm sure you'll understand. *(He points toward the table at which the four other men are seated)*

The gentleman to the right is Caiaphas, our religious leader, and you would say a man with political clout. Not a bad man, really, and shrewd. To his right is Simon the Pharisee. Then there is Josephus, a leading Sadducee, Nicodemus, a Pharisee who went to see Jesus at night, and myself. There were more of us, of course, but this will give you the idea. The debate's already started.

*Caiaphas:* But gentlemen. His having the people on his side is precisely our problem. The people are listening to him and he's undermining our God-given authority. His name calling of the Pharisees is inexcusable, and his attack on the temple was a blatant act of terrorism. Then, of course, there's Pilate. You know how he feels about local heroes! It's a matter of time before he starts to squeeze us. If we give him the least excuse he'll disband the council and destroy the temple. It could be the end of our nation.

We have to take immediate, decisive action in this affair. We've tried to stop him, but he ignores our warnings. We've tried to discredit him, but he talks down our scribes and lawyers. I don't see that we have any choice but to have him executed.

Still, I don't like it. It's the wrong time of year and the city's crawling with Galileans here for the Passover. The situation could become very nasty.

*Jonah:* I agree. You'll never take him. The people won't allow it. And if you catch him, you'll never make a charge stick.

*Josephus:* Never, Jonah, is a defeatist word. Every man has his price. Ask Simon about his dinner party last week.

*Simon:* I'd rather not discuss it. It was all very embarrassing. One of his women friends came and made a disgusting spectacle of herself, and when we asked her to leave, he abused us. Very unpleasant. It ruined the evening. But I heard one of his disciples muttering about Jesus being too slow to take power. Judas joined him because he thought Jesus was the Messiah, but now he's disillusioned. For a price he'd probably give us verbatim evidence that he claims to be the Messiah and specific information about when and where he can be picked up.

*Josephus:* If worst comes to worst, I know a few more former followers who for a small consideration will testify against him.

*Nicodemus* (angrily): And you'd break one of God's commandments! By bearing false witness you desecrate our tradition. Does our law judge a man without first giving him a hearing and learning what he does? No matter what his misdemeanours he deserves a fair trial.

*Jonah:* I agree with Nicodemus. This man *may* be a prophet as the people claim. We are responsible for the welfare of God's people. To kill one of God's messengers would be shameful. Perhaps we should consider the problem more carefully before we take any irreversible steps.

*Josephus:* "Prophet?" Jonah you have to be joking! You know as well as I do the kinds of people he hangs out with: criminals, prostitutes. He's a glutton and a drunk. When it suits him, he ignores or breaks the law. What prophet in the

whole of our history has behaved like this? He's not a prophet. He's a mad man, a fool with too much charisma for his
own good.

*Caiaphas:* Gentlemen, we're getting off the point. We're all
reasonable men, and I think most of us have learned that life
is a compromise. The fact is that if we don't do something,
our positions will soon be in jeopardy, and if he continues to
stir up the people, there could be mass Roman reprisals. As
leaders, we're responsible for the lives of our people and for
our holy covenant with God. It's better that one man should
die than that our whole nation be in danger. It's a question of
choosing the lesser of two evils. But may I remind you that
this is a very abrasive young man who's determined to meddle
in affairs that are none of his business. I think we should
bring the matter to a vote.

*Josephus:* One small point, Caiaphas. There's a rumour out
that if he's killed he'll rise from the dead.

*Caiaphas:* Thank you Josephus. I'll see that suitable precau-
tions are taken, possibly a guard put on the body. (Sar-
castically) The last thing we need is a resurrected hero.
*(Jonah gets up from the table and goes down into the
congregation.)*

*Jonah:* So you can see how it was. Nicodemus bought a hundred denarii worth of burial spices; that represents a lot of
Canadian dollars. Joseph of Arimathea, who also sat on the
council, went and secretly asked for Jesus' body, and we
buried it in his garden. Giving Jesus a decent burial was the
least we could do. As for the truth of the rumours of his
resurrection, I really couldn't say.

So thank you for your attention, good people, and have a
pleasant day (Or "May I wish you a very good evening?").

*The men leave and two women come out of the congregation,
sit down at the table and pick up the two coffee mugs.*

*Jenny:* Watching that Central American business on TV really *bothers* me. All that killing and torture! I don't understand
how people can do those sorts of things to each other.

*Clare:* I know. I can't watch it or I have nightmares. But

thank God I don't have to. It's a long way away.

*Jenny:* Heather's always firing off letters for Amnesty International and to MP's. I don't know how she does it. I don't have time to keep up with my own correspondence, let alone write to a dictator!

*Clare:* Right now, Jan's running around selling coffee from Nicaragua. She says it puts money in the pockets of the Nicaraguans and not the Americans. But it's so inconvenient for me to get and it costs more. Besides, my one pound of coffee isn't going to save the world and my time's valuable. I've got a family to look after. You can get so caught up in these things that you end up neglecting your own family.

*Jenny:* I think if you're going to get involved you really have to understand the issues, and I just don't have that kind of expertise.

*Clare:* You're right. We shouldn't feel guilty about it. There really isn't much we can do anyway.

REVIEW

Read the Bible passages: Mark 11: 15-18 and Luke 6: 27-31, and the summary below.

SUMMARY

For many Christians in the world today, Jesus' attitude to politics and violence is a crucial issue.

Jesus in some ways was like many modern revolutionaries. He defended the common people. He confronted the religious/political authorities of his day. He was on the run and in hiding. He was falsely arrested, tortured, and given a death usually reserved for revolutionaries. There was something fiercely, determinedly smouldering within him. But he never led a revolt or killed anyone. What kind of revolutionary was he?

We can best see his political relationships in his arrest, trial and execution. The final charge against him was that he claimed to be a Messiah-King; the Romans carried out the execution.

It's possible, considering Pilate's ruthless reputation, that it was primarily he who wanted Jesus killed. Jesus himself probably disliked the Romans as much as anyone, and in a number of gospel stories it seems evident he was tempted by political power. Yet perhaps because the people did not see him for the kind of Messiah he was, he firmly rejected it.

According to the gospel writers, the local authorities wanted Jesus killed. Jesus saw and confronted them as the real oppressors. In these stories the local authorities betray Jesus to the occupying forces, and Judas betrays Jesus to them.

One might say Jesus was caught up in a web of institutionalized violence, but it is also certain he knew what he was doing. Jesus thought of himself as a prophet, a breed quite distinct from revolutionaries. He was called to proclaim God's message and suffer the consequences. But he also thought of himself as more than a prophet, and his death as having a unique significance. His death was a "ransom for many" for the forgiveness of sins.

Jesus' sayings on violence often seem contradictory and mustn't be taken out of context. His basic ethic was love, not non-violence. Although violence must always remain abhorrent, it cannot be absolutely ruled out for Christians.

As for Jesus' attitude to our political problems today, what can be said with certainty is that he would never be found sitting quietly on the sidelines.

SMALL GROUP DISCUSSION

*Track A*

1. Have two members of your group continue a debate between Nicodemus and Caiaphas. Nicodemus might argue that human life is always precious, and when one person's rights are endangered everyone's rights are endangered; Caiaphas, that occasionally an individual may have to be sacrificed for the good of the whole group. They might give current illustrations for their viewpoints.

2. To what extent were men like Jonah in the play caught up in the workings of a system and so not to be condemned

as individuals? What other options did they have?

The women at the end of the play give lack of time, lack of expertise and family obligations as reasons for not involving themselves with people unjustly condemned and impoverished today. These are arguments most of us from time to time raise. To what extent are they valid? How do we decide what time and thought we should put into justice and social action issues?

3. In the film *Missing* a young American journalist living in Chile disappears during the 1973 coup there, and his father and wife search for him. They eventually learn that he was tortured and killed by the new Chilean government but with the agreement of American officials. He knew too much. If he reported the CIA involvement in the overthrow of the democratically elected (but socialist) government of Allende there would be an outcry. But American business men (and consequently the American government) felt they had to replace Allende's government with one more sympathetic to their interests. When confronted with the facts, an American official seriously argues that the journalist had to be killed in order to protect the more than 3,000 American companies operating in Chile and the profits which make for "a damn good way of life," - the American way of life.

a. Might a similar desire to protect Jewish culture, religion and economics (or for Pilate, Roman economics) have been a strong motivation for killing Jesus?

b. The CIA interference in Chile feels very like the brutality of Pilate in Palestine. Are there similarities between the Roman involvement in Palestine, the American hold on Central and South America, and the Soviet presence in Eastern Europe? What might they be?

4. Louis Riel has lived in Canadian history as both a traitor and a folk hero. His passionate defense of the land rights of the Metis (Indian-French people) led him to open rebellion against the British in the Red River region. The rebellion quelled, he was publicly hanged as a murderer.

a. In what ways did Riel resemble Jesus?

b. How do you see Jesus reacting in a situation such as Riel's?

5. Jesus at the last supper refers to "my blood of the covenant shed for many for the forgiveness of sins." Do you see Jesus as having died *for you?* Does his death affect your life?

*Track B*

Read Mark 11: 11-18.

1. What is the significance of verse 2?

2. What does Jesus mean when he says that the temple has been made into a "den of robbers?" What was his main objection to what was going on there (See the text, p. 79)?

3. Why did the authorities *fear* him for this action? Using the text of this book, discuss how this incident in the temple placed Jesus in a dangerous position as a kind of revolutionary.

Read Luke 6: 27:31. Read *Solentiname* Appendix V (perhaps silently, because of the length).

4. These commands of Jesus seem rather impractical for everyday life. Do you think Jesus meant them always to be carried out or only in certain circumstances? Can you think of some circumstances where turning the other cheek would not be the right or loving thing to do? Are there circumstances where turning the other cheek would be best?

5. Do you agree with the people of Solentiname that turning the other cheek means "not to fight for yourself but for others?"

6. In your experience, is it true that turning the other cheek is "a way of appealing to good that's in the hearts of the most evil of people?" To what extent might this depend on the character of the enemy?

ALTERNATIVE PROGRAM

As an alternative to Track A or B you may decide to use the

film *Khotso* (Peace), which portrays the struggle of two Christian leaders in the South African Council of Churches against the apartheid system. The film contains forceful statements on the revolutionary character of the Christian faith. Read the following questions in the group before viewing the film.

1. Bishop Tutu often speaks of institutional violence. In this film he says, "The system tries all it can to destroy us. It won't succeed."

   a. Why is it *the system* and not individual people who are enemies of black South Africans?

   b. There is only a ripple of protest against apartheid throughout the world. It is mainly North American and European companies, through their investments and use of South African cheap labour and mineral resources that keep that country in business. We are benefitting from the system that Bishop Tutu refers to. Are we then in any way responsible for it?

2. Bishop Tutu encourages disinvestment in South Africa. How does he argue in the film against those who say the blacks will be hurt most by disinvestment?

3. Speaking of the Bible, Bishop Tutu says, "It is the most revolutionary thing around. Well maybe they (the missionaries) shouldn't have brought it, because quite frankly, we are taking it seriously." Do you agree that the Bible is a revolutionary document?

4. There are many depressing scenes in this film, but in what ways is it a hopeful statement?

FEEDBACK

WORSHIP

*A Hymn*
No. 460 (Were you there?) or No. 468 (The strife is o'er)
Members of the group may lead in prayers of intercession for
- the countless innocent people who, like Jesus, are detained, tortured and executed today
- those who struggle with great self-sacrifice in movements to

change unjust and dehumanizing social and economic systems
- those who find their integrity compromised by systems and structures over which they have little control.

In a moment of silence members may meditate on their own personal commitments to justice.

Stand in a circle with joined hands. Let the leader close with Bishop Matthew's blessing:

May the Lord Jesus Christ, who walks on wounded feet,
walk with you to the end of the road.
May the Lord Jesus, who serves with wounded hands,
help you to serve each other.
May the Lord Jesus, who loves with a wounded heart,
be your love forever.
Bless God wherever you go,
And may you see the face of the Lord Jesus
In everyone you meet.

# THE SEVENTH SESSION

PURPOSE:

1. To see how Jesus, himself risen from death, leads us from ways of death to ways of life.
2. To see how in the past Jesus has given new life to the Church, and to discern new shoots of life today.

OPENING PRAYER

ACTIVITY FOR THE WHOLE GROUP*

All the members can check the following questions in their own books, and then for fifteen or twenty minutes talk together in groups of three about why they made these choices.

1. Since I've done this study, when I think of Jesus, I think of (Circle two or three)
    a. A man with great spiritual power
    b. His love for the poor and sinners
    c. A man who enjoyed people's company
    d. A man who was unjustly and cruelly killed
    e. The person in whom God was uniquely present
    f. A man who thought highly of women

*Adapted from *Serendipity,* published by Serendipity House, Creative Resources, © 1978 Serendipity House.

g. A man who wasn't afraid to balk at authority

h. Other

2. If Jesus were alive today and a citizen of our country, I think he would probably (Circle one)

a. Leave

b. Get involved in politics

c. Be a radical

d. Work through the church

e. Work outside the church

f. Identify with minority causes

g. Move away for a few years to let God help him "get it together."

h. Settle down and become an average citizen

i. Other

3. Since doing this study I can honestly say that my faith commitment to Jesus Christ is (Circle one)

a. Weaker

b. Stronger

c. Growing

d. Up for grabs

e. About the same

f. Just starting

g. Something I want to make but I don't know where to begin

4. If I knew I could count on the support of others in my group or family I would like to

a. Talk to my friends and neighbours about Jesus

b. Get involved in making things right in the world

c. Volunteer for missionary service

d. Alter my life-style

e. Get serious with God

f. Other

REVIEW

Read the Bible passages: Matthew 27: 45-50 and Acts 5: 27-42, and the summary below.

SUMMARY

The Cross for us has many facets: a young man unjustly killed, the forgiveness of God, a bit of light on human suffering. It reminds us of Jesus' strength, his spirituality, of why he died. As for the resurrection we can only weigh in the evidence, the words and actions of the first Christians, the existence of the Christian Church itself.

Some of our Third World sisters and brothers have very different insights into the Cross and resurrection than our traditional Western ones. They see God as the suffering, powerless God of the Cross. To be with God is to be with the suffering and powerless of the world. The resurrection rehabilitates Jesus. He is not a criminal, but God with us. The resurrection is the political defeat of those who killed Jesus, and eventually means the defeat of all those like them. It requires the poor to practise political activity, for in the end they must win. The resurrection means that God is ultimately in control of the world, and God's Kingdom is growing now in the struggles of history. It means an end to fear, courage for this life, and hope for a life to come. Because of the enormous love it reflects we can know that we will be saved by grace and so can afford to take moral risks. And finally, the resurrection makes Christ's Spirit available to people of all time.

These people are working out the meaning of the Cross and resurrection in their own situation, as has gone on in the church from the beginning. Our traditions also reflect these same patterns of suffering and renewal. The denominations which make up the roots of The United Church of Canada have a history of stress on the Spirit, modesty of living, simplicity of worship and social justice. Other traditions have their own distinctive patterns of revival.

But all new shoots with time become dusty, and few would deny that the Church at this moment, the whole Church, is ready for a fresh vision of what it is about. The question is, can it catch from Jesus the vision and strength to be an effective agent for good in a problem-racked world. Can we reach out and take Jesus' offer of life?

SMALL GROUP DISCUSSION

*Track A*

1. The following are the first and last stanzas of John Updike's poem "Seven Stanzas at Easter":

Make no mistake: if He rose at all
it was as His body;
if the cells' dissolution did not reverse,
the molecules reknit, the amino acids rekindle,
the Church will fall.

Let us not seek to make it less monstrous,
for our own convenience, our own sense of beauty,
lest, awakened in one unthinkable hour,
we are embarrassed by the miracle,
and crushed by remonstrance.*

a. Are there ways in which we try to make the resurrection more manageable and "less monstrous," try to soften its impact on our lives?
b. If it could be proved that the resurrection never happened, would the Church fall?
c. If it could be proved the resurrection never happened, how would this affect your own beliefs about
- the goodness of God
- who controls the world
- eternal life
- the divinity of Jesus
- the forgiveness of sins?
2. The Chinese theologian Choan-Seng Song says, "The resurrection is a politics that makes an opening in a dead end " (*Third-Eye Theology,* p. 257). In what ways do you see the resurrection making "openings" for people in the Third World?
3. Within your group, map out a scenario for the future of the church. What do you see happening in the local, national, and international church in fifty years' time? What would you like to see happening? What issues or

emphases should the church be concentrating on now?

*Track B*

Read again Matthew 27: 45-50.

1. "The endless mystery of why we suffer and die. But he has suffered and died with us and so we do not suffer and die alone. We are not abandoned."

a. How does the suffering of Jesus help us to understand why there is so much terrible suffering in the world, in spite of the goodness of God?

b. Does the despair of Jesus mean anything to you when you feel forsaken in the circumstances of life?

Read again Acts 5: 27-42.

2. Consider the courage of the apostles to disobey the authorities by continuing to preach the risen Christ.

a. What accounts for their courage to risk beating, imprisonment and death? (Refer to the text on the Politics of the Resurrection, p. 89).

b. Under what circumstances is it right for a Christian to disobey the law?

3. Note the advice of the Pharisee Gamaliel to the council that the apostles should not be killed (verses 33-39). Why were the followers of Jesus not "scattered" and why did their movement not "come to nothing" when Jesus was killed (as in the case of the followers of Theudas and Judas of Galilee)?

4. On what basis can we today continue to believe in the resurrection of Jesus?


FEEDBACK


EVALUATION

For about ten minutes in groups of three discuss with each other:

- a few of the main things you have learned during the study
- things you would like to have learned, and
- areas in which you would like to go on learning or actions you would like to take as a result of the study.

WORSHIP

*A Hymn*
No. 253 (Be Thou my vision) or No. 30 (Praise my soul)
The leader may ask the group what prayer concerns they
have, especially what they would give thanks for. The leader
can invite group members to pray for each other's concerns
and to offer thanks in the few minutes that follow.
Let the whole group say together the following creed, reading
it over first in silence.

We believe in a loving God, creator of all humankind
who forms and sustains the universe in power and love.
We believe in a God who has not divided people
into the owners and the slaves, the poor and the rich,
specialists and the ignorant.
We believe in Jesus Christ, God incarnate,
who showed us by His words and work,
His suffering with others
and His conquest of sin and death,
what human life ought to be and what God is like.
We believe in the Spirit who came with Jesus
into the world,
who is present with us now and always,
and can be experienced in prayer, in action, in forgiveness,
in the Word, and in the fellowship of the church.
We believe in the community of all peoples
and in our responsibility for making our world
into either a place of misery, hunger and tyranny,
or into the City of God.
We believe that it is possible to build a just peace,
We believe that a life full of meaning is possible for all,
and in the future of this world of God. Amen.*

While the group stands in a circle with clasped hands, let the
leader close with the following benediction (taken from the
United Church Service Book):

*Creed adapted from a poem by German theologian Dorothy Sölle, and
the Latin American credo, used in a service of remembrance and prayer for
the suffering in Central America on the anniversary of the death of
Archbishop Oscar Romero, Centenary United Church, Hamilton, Ont. 1982.

Go into the world
With a daring and tender love.
The world is waiting.
Go in peace.
And all that you do
Do it for love,
And by the Spirit of Jesus
Who is the Lord.

# APPENDIX

# THE WEDDING AT CANA

The man in charge of the party
tasted the water that had turned to wine,
without knowing where it was from;
only the servants knew,
for they had drawn the water.

*John 2:1-12*

*Oscar:* "It seems to me that the wine means joy, a party. To be happy. Enjoyment. Also love. He wanted to make us see that he was bringing enjoyment, happiness, a party."

*Olivia:* "Joy. And also unity. Wine unites. He was coming to bring about unity among people. But liquor can separate too, and lead to quarrels, stabbings..."

*Angel:* "Also, when rich people drink liquor in selfish parties, it doesn't create any unity. There's no brotherhood there — at least, for the people who are being excluded..."
I said that in the Old Testament the messianic era had often been described as an epoch of great abundance of wine. The prophet Amos had said that when the Messiah came there would be great harvests of wheat and grapes, and that the hills would distill wine. Isaiah says that God was going to prepare a banquet for all the peoples, with very good meat and very good wines. And he had also prophesied about the Messiah, saying that "he would not be sad." By this miracle Christ is making it clear that he is the promised Messiah.

*Marcelino:* "We see then that he was coming to bring unity and brotherhood among people. That's the wine he brought. If there's no brotherhood among people there's no joy. Like a party where people are divided, where they don't all share alike, it's a party without joy. A person's birthday or saint's day is not a happy party if there's division..."

"Or if they stab each other," said *Andrea,* Oscar's wife.

*Marcelino* went on: "So a society with quarrels, with social classes, can't have a true banquet, a true party."

*William:* "The party will be the kingdom of God, that new society. And that's why Christ, when he said goodbye to his disciples at the Last Supper, he told them that he wouldn't drink wine any more until he drank it with them in that kingdom."

*Jose Alaniz,* Olguita's husband: "I think we should ask for wine for everybody, like Christ taught us to ask for bread in the Our Father. Bread and wine are equally important. Bread is the food and wine is the joy, and that's why he made one miracle with bread and another with wine. Because there are so many poor people, who don't have any parties, drunken brawls maybe, but not joy. The joy of the kingdom will come when everybody loves each other and everybody is friends."

*Teresita,* William's wife: "But it wasn't at any old party that he performed the miracle. It was at a wedding party."

*Olguita:* "The wedding meant that he was coming to bring love."*

*From *The Gospel in Solentiname,* by Ernesto Cardenal, Vol. I, trans. D.D. Walsh, Maryknoll, Orbis Books, 1976, selections from pp. 154-157.

# COME TO ME AND REST

Come to me,
all you who are weary of your labours
and your burdens,
and I will give you comfort.

*Matthew 11:25-30*

*Felipe:* "I think he's seeing the suffering of the people more than anything else. We bear the burden of exploited people too... And I think this is the burden Jesus is talking about, and that he wants to ease."

*The Teacher:* "Undoubtedly he doesn't call the rich and powerful but the people who have burdens. It's a call to the exploited from everywhere, seeing also that they're weary of their labours. In those days the world was full of slaves, and it's just the same today, except that they're called workers. To all of them he offers comfort."

*Carlos:* "This comfort he offers is not for tomorrow but for today. And he gives this comfort through struggle. And it's not that the poor are going to live like the rich but instead with a new sense of life that the people who cling to their wealth can never know."

*Alvaro Guzman:* "He's come to free people with burdens, people overwhelmed by the weight of all the dictatorships of the earth. He's brought love so that he's the one who governs us and so that he organized all human life, putting an end to exploitation, giving us the comfort of no more injustice."

> Because my yoke is soft
> And my burden is light.

*Alvaro:* "His yoke is the only one that's not slavery but freedom: freedom from sin, freedom from oppression, freedom from everything. We've been talking here about simple people and humble people and poor people. It's them that Jesus calls to, to the ones who are tired of their burdens, so that they can find 'rest' in him — the solution to all their problems."

*Julio:* "And the yoke he offers them is a new social system based on love. Their burden is to live together in a community of love, and that's a burden easy to bear. 'Submit to my liberation,' he's saying."*

---

*From *The Gospel in Solentiname,* by Ernesto Cardenal, Vol. II, trans. D.D. Walsh, Maryknoll, Orbis Books, 1978, selections from pp. 13-16.

# RICHES

---

Notice and beware of all greed;
for people's lives do not depend
on the many things they may have.

*Luke 12:13-21*

---

*Olivia:* "Happiness doesn't depend on riches. There are many rich people that are unhappy."

*Mariita:* "It's the riches that make them unhappy. They have worries we don't have."

*I:* "According to Jesus, it's not just happiness; it's life itself that doesn't depend on the things one may have."

*Tomas:* "A selfish person is dead in the midst of life."

*Marcelino:* "Life depends on food, clothing, also housing, medicine. But he says not 'on the many things they may have': that's to be rich."

*Felipe:* "The many things (having too much), that's what kills life."

*Rebeca,* Marcelino's wife: "The fact that some people have too much of a lot of things, that makes for law suits, wars, that also kills life."

*William:* "He's also saying that life doesn't depend on *having;* it depends on *being.*"

*Teresita:* "So that's why he didn't want to give that man the riches he was fighting for, they aren't any good."

*Laureano:* "As I understand it, he says that having riches isn't living, it's being isolated, it's death."

*Olivia:* "He shows that riches are the same as greed. Because he talks about riches and before he said 'beware of greed.' Because the richer you are the greedier you have to be. And then it's death, not happiness; so riches are a curse."

*Alejandro:* "Riches that are shared unevenly."

*Donald:* "He was showing the one who was asking him this that he shouldn't be selfish. Because he *was* being selfish. He wouldn't let the brother alone who had the things. And then, instead of abandoning that system, he wanted to be another greedy man, or he'd become one. They'd be two greedy men fighting over an inheritance."*

*From *The Gospel in Solentiname,* by Ernest Cardenal, Vol. III, trans. D.D. Walsh, Maryknoll, Orbis Books, 1979, selections from pp. 115-117.

# DO NOT JUDGE OTHERS

How can you see the mote in your brother's eye
and not see the beam that is in your own eye?
How can you say to your brother:
"Brother, let me remove the mote that is in your eye?"
Hypocrite! First take out the beam from your eye
and you will thus be able to see well
to take out the mote from your brother's eye.

*Luke 5: 37-42*

*Donald:* "You can always see clearly the evil in others and not the evil in yourself. But this is not seeing clearly. Because if you have a beam in your eye you're not seeing anything."

*Oscar:* "You see the other person's error and not your own (or *my* own, I mean; why should I say 'you'?). And that's an error that I commit. Maybe bigger than the error that I'm looking at. It's the same as I was saying before, about judging: the way I judge I'm judged. Because if I judge bad I make myself evil. Noticing somebody else's speck is judging him, is seeing him evil, and that makes me worse. Because I don't do it to reform him but because I think I'm better, and therefore I'm worse. I'm a blind man who wants to guide others when I have a beam in my eye and how am I going to remove a speck when I can't see...Well, I'm all mixed up, let somebody else talk."

*Manuel:* "The hypocrites are the Pharisees, right? And the Pharisees were the guides of the people, right? Then the blind guides are the hypocrites who want to reform others without reforming themselves. The disciples of Jesus may be Pharisees, and the revolutionaries may be Pharisees, if they don't criticize themselves."

*Julio:* "I've been talking against the rich, but I see that what's here can be applied to the poor as well: not to blame everything on the rich, because maybe the poor are just alike, except that they don't do some things because they can't. So first we ought to change ourselves so that later we can demand that the rich change themselves."

*William:* "This is an important call for self-criticism. Also for criticism, because you can remove the mote from your brother if your eye is clean. Here in the Youth Club there's a lot of criticism and self-criticism. After they've had a party, for instance, they examine what things were bad and what were good, what was positive and what was negative."

"Is that all?"

"We've seen it all clearly," said *Milagros.*

When the comments were over I informed them that we had learned that one of the people present in the church (Mario, the schoolteacher) was a spy. We had also learned that his real name wasn't Mario and that he wasn't a teacher but a captain in the army. He changed colour, protested with a lot of false starts that he was not a spy but a revolutionary. I insisted that we had proof. But that we were not judging him or condemning him.

*Felix* said: "What does it matter if he's in the secret police, if that's how he earns his living? As long as he doesn't lie."

*Mariita:* "As long as he just says what he sees and hears. Because this is the gospel, and we say it publicly.''*

---

*From *The Gospel in Solentiname,* by Ernesto Cardenal, Vol. II, trans. D.D. Walsh, Maryknoll, Orbis Books, 1978, pp. 129-131.

# THE OTHER CHEEK

---

If someone strikes you on one cheek,
offer him also the other cheek.
And if someone takes your coat from you,
let him have your shirt also.

*Luke 6: 27-31*

---

*Julio Ramon,* incredulous: "Does this mean that the poor person must suffer and let people take his things away from him?"

*Laureano:* "It seems to me that this applies to the rich: they should let people take their things from them. He talks about a coat, right? And poor people are always in shirtsleeves (laughter). So when the revolution comes and their farms are taken away, their factories, their extra houses, they shouldn't put up any resistance. And if they lose one piece of property, let them offer up the other piece."

*Felipe:* "Let them give it up freely and give more than is asked of them. This is for the haves. What can the poor give, if they don't have anything? The Christian should be detached from everything, not wanting to defend property with force."

*Manuel:* "Then what it says about the other cheek is only for the rich, and the poor should never turn the other cheek?"

*I said:* "This is also a precept for the poor, and it is very revolutionary. I mean that we must pass over our own personalities, put aside all personal pride and all individualism, fight not for our own interests but for those of other people. This doesn't mean not to fight. It means not to fight for yourself but for others. And Christ says to turn the other cheek, but it's *your* other cheek, not the other cheek of other people. Christians who don't fight for the revolution aren't turning either one of their two cheeks. They're turning the cheeks of undernourished children, of abandoned widows, of workers robbed of their work.''

*William:* ''And I believe that in the revolutionary struggle, turning the other cheek, your own other cheek, is also a very effective weapon. It's a way of appealing to the good that's in the hearts of the most evil of people. And something like this happened here with that guard who was bothering us so much because of what we were saying in these meetings and he kept on saying that he was going to screw us because we were Communists. The boys and girls of the Youth Club went and talked to him in a friendly way. They treated him with love, and he changed. Not right away. At first he denounced them to the commanding officer at San Carlos, saying that a group of young people had gone to his house to attack him. And he went on saying bad things about all of us. The group went back again. They told him he was poor like them, one of the exploited. And he admitted that he was, that he was very badly paid. Now, even though he's not in that post, now he's even our friend. And it was clear that at heart he was not an evil person. He was a guy who thought he had to be evil because he was a guard. And when he saw some friendly human beings, who didn't answer him with hatred, he changed, and his bad will toward us disappeared. This too is blessing those who curse us, doing good to those who hate us.''*

*From *The Gospel In Solentiname,* by Ernest Cardenal, Vol. II, trans. D.D. Walsh, Maryknoll, Orbis Books, 1978.

# FACE OF A POOR GOD

1. Face of a poor God
   Grieving, shamed, dying
   Look on your people
   In their distress
   Wipe all their tears
   Untwist coils of power
   Remould the structures
   Which keep us oppressed

2. Jesus who laughed then
   Give us the courage
   To feel the hurting
   Of a crushed world
   But through the hunger
   Pain and injustice
   To know that you will
   Laugh here again

3. Jesus who promised
   Life in its richness
   Waken us often
   Blow through our midst
   Give us your Spirit
   Recklessly loving
   Joy in the struggle
   Peace on the way

4. Give us a vision
   Whole, shining,
   glorious
   Of this world's peoples
   Gathered today
   Round the earth's table
   Feasting and singing
   God is victorious
   Praise to God's Name

Words by Patricia Wells

Tune: Bunessan
Traditional Gaelic melody
Arrangement by Evelyn McCulloch

# A RULE OF THUMB
# LIFE-STYLE CHECK LIST

WHY CHANGE?
1. To attempt some measure of solidarity with the world's poor; to avoid exploitation of them; to have more to give.
2. To preserve the environment.
3. For our own spiritual and physical well-being.

FOOD
- Emphasize the natural: fresh fruits, vegetables, whole grains rather than the processed
- Reduce the stimulants (tea, coffee, sugar)
- Eat low on the food chain: grains and legumes over against meat
- Eat foods in season rather than imports: read the labels, and don't hesitate to ask where something comes from
- Eat less (1.6 million Canadians are grossly obese)
- Consider a rule of no second helpings unless there are guests, but make the children's first helping generous
- Eat in restaurants only on rare occasions
- Grow your own
- Compost all your organic scraps
- Buy direct from the producer wherever possible.

CLOTHING
- Buy fewer, but quality items that will last: strenuously resist being enslaved to fashion
- Emphasize natural fibres (wool and cotton) or blends over pure synthetics

- Recycle: exchange children's clothes with other families; organize a clothing exchange at your church; trade a blouse or shirt you're tired of with a friend rather than buy a new one
- Scout out good second hand stores
- Sew, mend
- Plan to buy as much as possible on sale, but at a *real* sale, where you know the quality
- Patronize local businesses rather than outlets at large shopping malls unless the difference in price is very large (Consider the time and gas it takes to get there).

FURNITURE AND DECORATING
- Have a few beautiful things (they need not be expensive) but keep possessions to a modest level
- Recycle, reupholster, cherish old family possessions; don't buy for the sake of image.

ENERGY CONSUMPTION
- Sell your second car, make your present car last longer, organize a car pool, consider selling your car and using public transport
- Emphasize local and home-made recreation
- Question the number and size of your appliances; consider sharing freezers, lawn mowers, with other families
- Turn off lights, turn down your thermostat, consider turning off the heat in the spring and fall, and heating rooms as they are needed
- Use the cheapest and commonest source of fuel in your area
- Reduce to a minimum products that aren't renewable or bio-degradable (styrofoam, plastic, synthetics)
- Repair, recycle, insulate
- Begin to think in terms of "organic technology," e.g. small, sturdily built houses heated by the sun.

GENERAL
- Stress the nurturing of children, relationships with family and friends, rather than having or getting. It may mean working less and having less money to spend
- Entertain a wider circle of friends, but more simply

- Always laugh at advertising: before buying something consider whether it is a genuine need and not an advertising-created need, or a bowing to a certain social image
- Talk over with your children why you are spending the way you are (but don't expect them to agree and be prepared to make some reasonable compromises here)
- Put some of the money you save directly into a place where it can benefit the world's poor, e.g., The World Development, Service and Relief Fund; Mission and Service Fund
- Work out your life-style and make firm commitments within a group (family, friends, congregation); then make as many changes as possible together with other families
- See the world's people rather than your immediate neighbours and friends as your peer group.

QUESTION YOUR OWN LIFE-STYLE, NOT ANYONE ELSE'S
"AVOID SELF-DRAMATIZATION AND KEEP A STRONG SENSE
OF HUMOUR"*

*John V. Taylor, *Enough is Enough,* SCM Press, London, 1975, p. 80.

# CARDINAL RULES FOR MAKING CHANGE

1.The first rule of social change is: Don't take power personally. Meaning: (a) Don't bother doing it alone and (b) Don't get over-emotional.

2. Don't play Hamlet. He's on a head trip. He could not decide to be or not to be, so he decided by default. Not to decide and act is to decide and act in favour of the status quo, i.e., to resist change.

3. Only action counts. The score is not kept on feelings and emotions or profound ideas but on action that makes a difference.

4. Discontent is no sin. If you are contented, go chew your cud. Social change happens because a number of people are discontented and get organized and act.

5. Decide exactly what you want to get done. One single item is best. Two will bring more people in but dilutes it. Three gets fuzzy. You won't be able to remember four. Keep it exact, clear, so you can remember it if you go to jail.

6. Keep it simple so everybody, your people and your adversary, can't forget it.

7. Never make your adversary your personal enemy. He or she may join your group on the next issue. All people are respectable human beings. Pay respect to that humanity. "Love your adversary," says the Lord. But the Lord did not say love anything that person stands for or on. And don't give your adversary the excuse of making you a personal enemy.

8. Keep asking, "What are we doing?" Is this essential now, according to our plan, or is it a side track? Be able to answer what, why, when, where, how, who questions at all times.

9. Know your adversary well and his or her needs and wants, plans and goals. This is not to be manipulative. It is to help you know which item he or she will give up and which are non-negotiable.

10. Don't worry, plan. Worry is what people do about things they can't change. Of course, people will worry, and this must be handled with personal counseling and/or small-group work. This is important, but don't confuse it with action, change, or society.

APPENDIX IX

# ORGANIZATIONS RECOMMENDED IN TEXT

Amnesty International
(Concerning prisoners of conscience)
  Canadian Section
  P.O. Box 6033, Stn. J.
  Ottawa, ON, K2A 1TL

Bridgehead Trading
(An Alternative Marketing Organization)
  54 Jackman Ave.,
  Toronto, ON, M4K 2X5

Project Ploughshares
(Concerning Disarmament)
  Conrad Grebel College
  Waterloo, ON, N2L 3G6

Ten Days for World Development
  85 St. Clair Ave. E.,
  Toronto, ON, M4T 1M8
  (or the mission and development division of
  the Presbyterian, Anglican, United, Roman
  Catholic, or Lutheran Churches in Canada)

RECOMMENDED PERIODICALS

Central America Update
  Latin American Working Group,
  P.O. Box 2207, Station 'P'
  Toronto, ON, M5S 2T2

Fish Eye Lens
  Ecumenical Forum,
  11 Madison Ave.,
  Toronto, ON, M5R 2SR

GATT-fly Report,
  11 Madison Avenue,
  Toronto, ON, M5R 2SR

One World
  World Council of Churches
  150 Rue de Ferney
  Geneva, Switzerland

The New Internationalist
  113 Atlantic Ave.,
  Brooklyn, New York, 11201, USA

Action Agendas
Bonnie Greene, Division of Mission in Canada
  85 St. Clair Ave. E.
  Toronto, ON, M4T 1M8
  This is a new mini-resource from the Division of Mission in Canada and the Division of World Outreach of The United Church of Canada. Published six to eight times a year, *Action Agendas* give information and suggestions for action around issues of human rights, economic justice, disarmament and peace, and energy. Subscription $5.00 per year.

For a more complete list of relevant periodicals and organizations in the various regions of Canada, write for *Development Education Survey,* Canadian Council for International Co-operation, 321 Chapel St., Ottawa, ON K1N 7Z2.

# AUDIO-VISUAL OUTLETS

103-1955 West 4th Ave.
Vancouver, BC
V6J 1M7

4744 - 99 St.
Edmonton, AB
T6E 5H5

120 Maryland St.
Winnipeg, MB
R3G 1L1

225 - 50th Ave.
Lachine, PQ
H8T 2T7

320 Elizabeth Ave.
St. John's, NF
A1B 1T9
(filmstrips only)

Box 1560
Sackville, NB
E0A 3C0
(Films only)

Note: Films and filmstrips can be rented on a one time basis or as part of a yearly subscription rate. Check with AVEL outlets for United Church and non United Church charges.

# THE AUTHORS

If you were to have dinner with Pat and Harold Wells and their four children Peter, Sarah, Matthew, and Andrew, you couldn't be quite sure who had put the chicken in the oven. The Wells practise what they preach, defying stereotypes and moving easily from one role to another as they pursue the task of living justly in our affluent society. Both natives of Hamilton, Ontario, they returned to the area in 1981 after living for five and a half years as United Church of Canada missionaries in Lesotho, southern Africa. Today, Harold is minister of East Plains United Church in Burlington, while Pat teaches English as a second language to newly arrived immigrants.

Pat graduated with a B.A. in English and History at McMaster before doing the Primary Specialist Course at Toronto Teacher's College. As well as teaching for two years in downtown Toronto, she has been heavily involved in Sunday school and adult education groups in various Ontario congregations. In Lesotho, Pat taught English, Religious

Studies, and Geography in a boys' high school.

Harold did his B.A. at McMaster, his B.D. at Emmanuel College, Toronto, and was ordained in 1966. After finishing his M.Th. in Systematic Theology in Edinburgh, he served the Jarvis Pastoral Charge, taught at St. Paul's College, Waterloo, then completed his Ph.D. at McGill in 1972. He was minister for four years in the Sudbury area. In Lesotho, Harold was chaplain and lecturer in Theology at the University of Lesotho and Morija Theological Seminary.

# THE ARTIST

Enrico Cumbo

Nancy Ruth Jackson has always worked with books. After attending art school in Hartford, Connecticut, and Toronto, she began her apprenticeship in the book trade by working as a production and design assistant in such companies as Little, Brown and Company, and MacMillans of Canada, eventually becoming a full-fledged book designer. She now works as a free lance book designer and illustrator, while at the same time exploring the art of wood engraving, her main interest as an artist.

Nancy Ruth lives in a Christian community in Toronto, where her major concern is to live as a Christian, a single woman, and a self employed craftswoman in a large city without sacrificing her faith, sanity, or sense of humour.

THE ENGRAVINGS

As Christians, we are heirs to an ancient tradition of symbolism and imagery - a tradition we too often neglect. It is both exciting and risky for an artist to sift through centuries of this visual richness, to try and find the images that will speak most effectively to the reader. One hopes to create ideal pictures, which, like the gospels themselves, are deeply rooted in the past, yet fresh and new.

For the engravings in this book, I have borrowed some very old images. In the illustrations for chapter one, for example, the four winged beasts are the early Christian symbols for the four gospels: Matthew, the winged man; Mark, the lion; Luke, the ox; John, the eagle. In other places, I have used modern images which may be more familiar. (Barbed wire may be the twentieth century's most enduring contribution to the language of symbolism.)

It would be tempting to try to explain all the pictures with words. They were, however, created to speak for themselves, and to speak clearly and joyfully.

N.R.J.